A Perceptive Images © Publication for
Mortons Media Group Ltd

Written compiled and edited by	Keith Langston
Picture Editor	Sue Mills
Additional editorial material	Les Green Brian Sharpe
Thanks are due to	Steve Blackburn and Bob Melling at Bombardier Transportation Crewe Works for their invaluable help.
Layout and design	Stuart Elding
Published by	Mortons Media Group Ltd, Media Centre, Morton Way, Horncastle, Lincolnshire LN9 6JR. Tel 01507 523456
Printed by	William Gibbons and Son, Wolverhampton
Cover picture	Crewe built Stanier Pacific No 6201 *Princess Elizabeth* pictured whilst hauling a special charter train at the Severn Valley Railway. *John F Stiles*

Published August 2006   ISBN: 0-9552868-0-8   ISBN: 978-0-9552868-0-3

CREWE
LOCOMOTIVE WORKS

More than *8250* locomotives were built at *Crewe* – they were all *built with Pride.*

For more than 150 years, locomotive building and railway engineering has taken place at Crewe Works in Cheshire. In September 2005 the charity organisation known as the Webb Crewe Works Charity Fund staged an event called The Great Gathering in order to celebrate and recognise the achievements of the many thousands of people who had spent their working years at 'The Works'. Never since the end of steam in the UK (1968) had such an impressive collection of railway motive power been put on display at a locomotive works.

It is now unfortunately a fact that the Cheshire 'Railway Town' is unlikely ever to figure again in the production of 'new build' locomotives, multiple units or other rail vehicles. However, the Crewe site, now operated by the French Canadian company Bombardier, still figures prominently in some future plans to service and re-equip the modern railway industry.

In 2006 the workforce occupying the site, which locals and railway enthusiasts still fondly call 'The Works', is by comparison a small one, numbering only 700 or so. This is a far cry from the period during and immediately after the Second World War, when the workforce reportedly swelled to a staggering 20,000!

To illustrate briefly the past value of the railways to Great Britain and to put into perspective the importance of Crewe Works, Government figures from a wartime (1943) railway census make fascinating reading.

There were at that time some 19,624 locomotives, 1,250,000 goods wagons, 45,838 passenger vehicles providing 2,655,000 seats, and some 10,000 horses collectively owned by the various railway companies. The total track-mileage including sidings was 50,958, of which 19,273 miles were logged as being route mileage, and they were controlled by 10,300 signal boxes. For suppliers the business potential was huge!

Ex-LMS Stanier Princess Coronation Class Pacific No 6233 *Duchess of Sutherland* is pictured at Bramshall, near Uttoxeter, en route to Crewe on 8 April 2006 at 08.37am.
David Gibson

The modern-day Crewe Works is mainly engaged in what could best be described as peripheral railway rolling stock engineering work. In June 2006 Bombardier Transportation announced that it had been awarded two major contracts by the train operating company First Group. Employing some 4000 staff at 24 centres in the UK, Bombardier values the new contracts at £53-million and £85-million respectively.

The first contract calls for the refurbishment of 405 High Speed Train (HST) trailer cars and that work is to be undertaken at the firm's sites in Derby and Ilford, with the newly completed refurbishment centre at Derby getting the lion's share of the work — 294 vehicles compared with Ilford's allocation of 111.

The second, and largest, contract has been awarded for the overhaul of HST bogies. First Great Western had (at the time of writing) a period of 10 years to run on its franchise and, during that time,

the £85-million-worth of bogie work will, say Bombardier, be carried out at Crewe Works.

Others intending to refurbish the originally Crewe-built HST power cars are the leasing companies Angel Trains and Porterbrook, but their plans do not include the works that developed the locomotives. They have declared their intention to spend £15-million to re-engine Great North Eastern Railways' (GNER) high-speed train fleet. That work, which calls for the replacement of the original Paxman Valenta diesel engines with new units, is scheduled to be carried out at the Loughborough works of Brush Traction.

In addition, the leasing companies plan to spend £27-million upgrading the associated HST carriages.

Bombardier currently carries out contracted 'coded' and crash-damaged repair work at its Crewe site on multiple units etc. For some time now discussions have been going on between the Canadian transportation engineering company's

George V class 4-4-0 locomotives (CJ Bowen-Cooke) under construction in Crewe's No 9 erecting shop. This is in all probability a posed shot, with each of the workers having been asked to hold their position while the exposure was taken. Note the two foremen in their bowler hats. c1910.

The National Railway Museum

managers and the workers at Crewe in an effort to secure a viable future for what is left of the once-great locomotive works.

Any assumptions or analysis of that process are best left for other forums. What can be said is that there is a great deal more positive satisfaction in celebrating the magnificent achievements of the past than there is in anticipating the hopes for the long-term future of 'The Works'!

With that in mind, the events of 10-11 September 2005 will almost certainly be remembered as the last great celebration of 'Made in Crewe'. There is a will on the part of many to see perhaps one more such event before any further downsizing or worse takes place. Given the possible imminent disposal of part of the current works real estate (and any subsequent development of it), a gathering on the scale of the

percentage population-wise as badly as anywhere else in the UK from the loss of employment potential in the engineering sector.

Including the neighbouring region and discounting 'trading under a name', the non-railway companies no longer looking to employ and train the youth of south Cheshire in big numbers for skilled jobs in engineering were all legendary British companies: Rolls-Royce Motor Cars, Fodens Motor Works, ERF Ltd. If you could quantify the collective engineering skills those firms and 'The Works' developed for the general good of the local area in particular and the UK in general, it would be a truly awesome amount!

The railway works at Crewe came into being in 1843 following the construction of the first main line in the country by the Grand Junction Railway. It was born out of an idea put forward by Joseph Locke, the great railway engineer.

In 1831, a five-mile long railway was opened to run between Warrington and Newton-le-Willows in Lancashire. It was the Warrington & Newton Railway and connected with the Liverpool & Manchester Railway at a place that was accordingly named Newton-le-Willows Junction. The line, which ran towards Warrington and the River Mersey, was seen as an ideal starting-point for a route to Birmingham and the Midlands.

A Bill was presented to, and subsequently passed by, Parliament on 6 May 1833 for the building of a railway called the Grand Junction Railway, a name it took from the aforementioned

last one would, say the charity committee, be logistically impossible to stage.

The past history of the site as a major railway engineering works is one of the world's greatest industrial success stories. Perhaps that fact is what makes the shrinkage and, God forbid, a possible closure, so hard to take. The town of Crewe, which grew around a railway junction at Monks Coppenhall, has, in the post-war period, suffered

junction. Coincidentally, on the same day a separately presented Bill was passed for the building of the London & Birmingham Railway. Those two acts in effect guaranteed the future of Crewe as a railway town.

The opening of the works was celebrated on 2 December 1843, when a grand ball and banquet was held in the then rapidly developing town. Crewe was, from that day forth, destined to be known as 'the railway town'. Not until much later, when Messrs Rolls and Royce commenced manufacturing motor cars at Pyms Lane, would the railway industry's claim to be the town's major employer be even slightly challenged.

Mr Locke's railway career is a distinguished one and not without its moments of history-making, for he was on the footplate of the Liverpool & Manchester Railway locomotive *Rocket* that killed William Huskisson at the opening of that railway on 15 September 1830. Huskisson was the Member of Parliament for Liverpool and a member of the Government, and he had alighted from his train to chat to the Prime Minister of the day, the Duke of Wellington, while that gentleman leaned out of his carriage window. Mr Huskisson either never heard nor saw the approaching locomotive, or just fatally misjudged its speed. He was struck and suffered injuries from which he later died, making

LNWR No 3020 *Cornwall*, a 2-2-2 locomotive built at Crewe in 1847 and preserved as part of the national collection, is pictured in 'The Works' with the directors' inspection saloon, c1900.
National Railway Museum

him the world's first railway passenger to be killed by a train.

The engineer Locke was born in 1805, the son of a colliery manager from Attercliffe, Sheffield. Following his education, he was articled to George Stephenson at Newcastle and, after completing his apprenticeship, he stayed on to work with his master during the construction of Liverpool & Manchester Railway.

His relationship with the redoubtable Stephenson was reputedly not the most placid of affairs, and the two finally fell out in a big way over differing interpretations of the survey results concerning the Edge Hill-to-Liverpool Lime Street tunnel.

Locke went into business on his own account and was soon engaged on the construction of a section of the Grand Junction Railway from near Warrington to Whitmore. On the back of his success in that work, he subsequently took over the building of the section to Birmingham, a task started, but then given up by his old master, George Stephenson. Locke's business developed quickly and he became associated with many great railway construction projects, both in the UK and elsewhere.

Locke was sole chief engineer of the Grand Junction Railway from 1835 to 1846, having been appointed when he was only 30. Although engaged mainly on construction and civil engineering work,

This 1913 picture shows some young gentleman apprentices under the supervision of the foreman engaged in the production of nuts and bolts.
For the period the working conditions look extremely tidy, giving rise to the question as to whether this, too, is a specially posed picture.
National Railway Museum

he kept himself involved on the mechanical engineering side. His strongest suit is recorded as having been his exceptional organisational skills.

The Grand Junction Railway, so closely associated with Crewe Works and the very reason for the town's existence, was a unique railway achievement, for it was finished not only on budget but also on time, thanks in no small measure to the tenacity and guiding hand of its chief engineer.

On 4 July 1837, a locomotive with the imaginative name *Wildfire* hauled the Grand Junction Railway's inaugural train between Birmingham and Liverpool. In those early days the GJR had its works at Edge Hill, adjacent to the Liverpool & Manchester Railway's running lines. That facility was in practical terms too small, and the railway's directors had for some time been on the lookout for an alternative location. They were thus receptive to a proposal from their chief engineer.

Joseph Locke suggested Crewe as a potential site for a new locomotive and rolling stock works for the

GJR. He also drew up the initial plans, formulated the construction estimates and ultimately supervised the organisation of the first Crewe locomotive works.

It was a custom-built facility that also led to the building of houses for its future workers for, at that time, the 'Great Junction' was indeed in the middle of a field. After the houses came the schools, chapels, churches, shops and, of course, the pubs. The town of Crewe grew rapidly around its locomotive works and to the north of the railway junction. Present-day rail travellers alighting at Crewe often show surprise at the station's distance from the town and, indeed, the railway engineering works.

The Cheshire Records Office has, as part of its comprehensive archive, a large, hand-drawn map showing the original junction at Monks Coppenhall. The map dates from 1839 and we are indebted to them for allowing us to reproduce that historic document elsewhere in this publication.

Forging a locomotive axle,
LNWR c1912.
National Railway Museum

Wheel turning: the top picture shows this operation in 1914 being carried out to a set of express locomotive wheels by an LNWR employee while the bottom picture shows the same operation (but with a smaller diameter wheel set) being undertaken by an LMS employee, possibly in the 1930s.

National Railway Museum

A Crewe Works 18in gauge locomotive. *Pet* is preserved and on display at the NRM, York. Author

Stanier Princess Royal 4-6-2 No 46203 *Princess Margaret Rose* was completed at Crewe in 1935. The locomotive is pictured back at the works 70 years later in 2005. Author

Just prior to the move from Edge Hill, and while William Barber Buddicom was locomotive superintendent, the GJR constructed a 2-2-2 engine called *Aeolus*, numbered 26. That outside cylinder, double-frame locomotive was to become the forerunner of an important class, which subsequently became known as the 'Old Crewe' type.

Mr Buddicom during the course of his employ developed further that design, in partnership with Joseph Locke, but he resigned his post in August 1841. He was replaced as Locomotive Superintendent by the Cornish locomotive engineer Francis Trevithick. The latter was therefore Locomotive Superintendent at the Grand Junction Railway when the London & North Western Railway came into being in June 1846. He went on to serve the Northern Division of the new company for several years.

With foresight, the GJR directors realised that Crewe was destined to become a major railway junction and saw it rightly as the place to be. However, history has judged Locke's plans for those early works harshly. They have been described variously as 'barely adequate for the Grand Junction Railway's needs' and also as the 'least far-seeing of all Mr Locke's railway construction contracts'.

Nevertheless, it is to him that we must credit the selection of Crewe as a railway locomotive building and engineering centre. He was without doubt a clever structural engineer who contributed a great deal to the development in general of Britain's rail system. He died in Moffat, Scotland, in September 1860, aged just 55.

Crewe Locomotive Works very quickly established itself as what, in modern terms, would have been described as a 'centre of excellence' for steam locomotive building, under LNWR rule, and was justifiably described by *The Railway Magazine* in 1913 as 'the most famous railway works in the world'. When initially established, 'The Works' employed 7,000 to 8,000 men and boys.

Like a good many relationships in the then-developing industrial world, the one between the once-quiet Cheshire backwater of Monks Coppenhall and the town of Crewe, which had evolved, was a very close one. For many years almost all local families had members who worked in either the locomotive works or on the railway.

If you lived locally and did not work there, the chances were that you in some part still relied on their success for the quality of your livelihood. The

Stanier mogul 2-6-0 No 42968, a preserved locomotive based at the Severn Valley Railway, was built at Crewe in 1934 and is seen back in 'The Works' 52 years later.
Author

life of the area and its people centred on the all-important works; as the factory was constructed so were streets of houses built nearby for the workers. The railway company in a way tried to provide for their employees' every need – indeed, they even built a church.

It was, of course, a railway works in the full sense of the word as, in addition to manufacturing locomotives and rolling stock, the facility produced hundreds of other items required by the world's burgeoning railway companies. Many railway bosses became councillors and, in later years, aldermen of the borough. The railway made the town and, in return, the town made the railway!

The products made at the works were very diverse, including steel rails, bricks, signal equipment, gas mantles and even soap made by reclaiming the grease from the dirty cloths returned for washing to the steam sheds by the locomotive crews. In fact the early Crewe Works ethos was 'never buy anything the works themselves can manufacture cheaper'.

The works became a training centre for hundreds of men, many of whom took the skills they had learned to all parts of the then-developing world. Thus the techniques originated at Crewe became accepted 'best practice' in railway workshops throughout the old British Empire and beyond.

In October 1843, the first locomotive actually built at Crewe Works was completed. It was numbered 32 and called *Tamerlane,* and in the December of that year a grand celebration ball and banquet was held to mark the occasion. In July 1845 the locomotive regarded by many as actually the first was rolled out. It was No 49 *Columbine* – the first 'Standard 6ft' with a 2-2-2 wheel arrangement.

In 1855 a great reorganisation and extension to the works took place that, in the main, solved the difficulties created by Locke's 'cramped' original plans.

The first of George Whale's 6ft four-coupled side-tank locomotives built in 1906. The class was intended for suburban work on the lines in and around London, Birmingham and Manchester. Crewe Works Archive

Welcome to Crewe Works. No 46203 on display at the main gate in September 2005. Author

Hardwicke seen on the turntable at the NRM. A Crewe-built loco, in service it ran return London-Manchester every day for 20 years, in which time it covered more than two-million miles. Author

In 1857 John Ramsbottom was appointed locomotive superintendent of the London North Western Railway, Northern Division, at Crewe. Significantly, in 1858 the DX Class 0-6-0 was introduced.

The engines were very successful and stayed in production until the early 1870s, with a total of 943 being built. They were at the time the most numerous class of locomotive in Britain. In December 1866, No 613 of the 0-6-0 DX class became the official 1000th locomotive to have been built at Crewe.

During Ramsbottom's watch the 18in gauge internal works railway was installed with its first steam engine, *Tiny,* which appeared in the spring of 1862. Later other narrow gauge locomotives were built to run on the system, among them *Pet, Nipper, Tipsy* and *Midge.*

Interestingly Mr Ramsbottom's successor, Francis William Webb, also ordered two more 18in gauge

engines to be built, and they were named *Billy* and *Dickie.* One of them found employment, albeit of a temporary nature, outside the confines of the works. In the 1890s a section of narrow gauge track was laid alongside the Middlewich branch of the Shropshire Union Canal and *Dickie* pulled six loaded coal-carrying narrowboats! The records do not say how successful, or otherwise, the ground-breaking experiment was.

In 1862 Mr Ramsbottom was appointed locomotive superintendent of the entire LNWR. Owing to ill-health, he retired in September 1871 and was replaced by FW Webb.

Webb is the man in whose name the laudable Crewe Works charity is set up. The works prospered extremely well under him, so much so that, in August 1876, the 2000th locomotive was completed, a Webb-designed 2-4-0 tank. Webb earned the title 'The King of Crewe', but who exactly was he?

Crewe Pacifics, left to right: *Princess Elizabeth, Princess Margaret Rose, Duchess of Hamilton.* Author

FW Webb – *The king of Crewe*

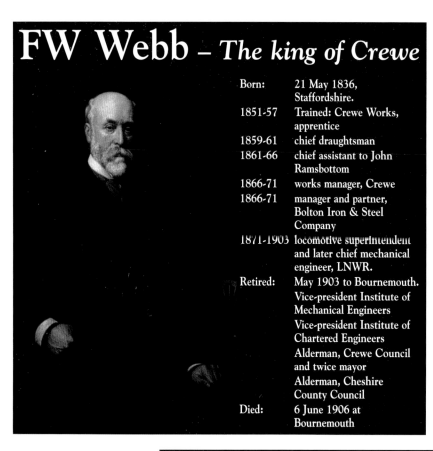

Born:	21 May 1836, Staffordshire.
1851-57	Trained: Crewe Works, apprentice
1859-61	chief draughtsman
1861-66	chief assistant to John Ramsbottom
1866-71	works manager, Crewe
1866-71	manager and partner, Bolton Iron & Steel Company
1871-1903	locomotive superintendent and later chief mechanical engineer, LNWR.
Retired:	May 1903 to Bournemouth. Vice-president Institute of Mechanical Engineers Vice-president Institute of Chartered Engineers Alderman, Crewe Council and twice mayor Alderman, Cheshire County Council
Died:	6 June 1906 at Bournemouth

The bare facts are, in themselves, an indication of the calibre of this great locomotive builder but, when you couple those with the additional information that he was responsible for 29 designs and the building of 2366 engines (more than a quarter the Crewe total), you begin to see why he justified the title 'King of Crewe'. He also was the first Crewe engineer to experiment with and then successfully build railway locomotives utilising the 'compound' system.

Historians have said that, although on occasions benevolent, Webb was autocratic and self-assured, stating that he 'ruled the works with a rod of iron'. He was also highly inventive and always willing to try out new ideas, but he ran a very tight ship to which he entirely dedicated his life. It is worthy of note that his apprenticeship at Crewe was served under Francis Trevithick, of the pioneering steam family.

Under his reign in June 1887, the works turned out its 3000th locomotive, an impressive 2-2-2-2 compound tank engine numbered 600. March 1900 saw the 4000th locomotive produced at the works, a Jubilee class four-cylinder compound 4-4-0 locomotive No 1926 and named *La France*.

It was under Webb's guidance that the LNWR

a classic LMS line-up

developed its famous class of 2-4-0 Precedent locomotives. They were nicknamed 'Jumbos' and were a development of John Ramsbottom's Newton Class, a design introduced in 1866. From 1874 Webb built a further 20 of these but incorporated many modifications, including higher boiler pressure.

In all Crewe built 166 of the locomotives, a process that ended in 1882. However, the whole Precedent class was renewed or refurbished between 1887 and 1902. They were highly successful, very reliable and extremely fast engines, much loved by the enginemen of the time.

During the so called 'Race for the North' (1895 version) between the railway companies operating on the East and West Coast routes to Scotland, the West Coast route was the stage for a particularly memorable performance by a Precedent.

The preserved example, No 790 *Hardwicke* (National Railway Museum) was chosen for the Crewe-Carlisle leg on the night of 22-23 August 1895 and the locomotive did extremely well. The route was a particularly punishing one for steam incorporating, as it does, the climb to Shap Summit. No 790 achieved a remarkable average speed of 67.2mph for the 141-mile journey.

Hardwicke went on to run return London-Manchester every day for 20 years, in which time it covered more than two-million miles, setting a record that has never been bettered. In 1923 the 'Jumbos' were taken into LMS ownership, and No 5001 *Snowdon* was the last of the famous class to be withdrawn in 1934.

Francis Webb introduced a class of 0-6-0 coal engines in 1873 and, from that design, the Webb 0-6-2T Coal Tank type of locomotive was developed. One of those venerable engines has made it into preservation and No 1054 is currently undergoing a comprehensive rebuild at the Ingrow works of the Keighley & Worth Valley Railway.

The locomotive was outshopped at Crewe in 1888 and it was the 250th of the 300 examples built over 16 years. It later carried the number 7799 while in LMS ownership, following the railway grouping of 1923. It was given the number 58926 when it came into British Railways ownership in 1948.

The historically important tank engine was withdrawn to store in 1939 but, because of the wartime shortage of locomotives, it was returned to service in 1940. It was a much-travelled engine and even had a spell working for the National Coal Board in Pontypridd. It was finally withdrawn for scrapping in 1958 (but then saved for preservation), having

Outside the running shed at Camden (1B), the pride of the LMS. Note that by this time (c1939), the foreman was no longer expected to wear a bowler but instead sported the more casual trilby. Left to right: Jubilee Class 4-6-0 No 5588 *Kashmir*, an unknown unrebuilt 4-6-0 Royal Scot Class locomotive, Streamlined Princess Coronation 4-6-2 No 6225 *Duchess of Gloucester*, an LNWR 4-6-0 Prince of Wales class and rebuilt Royal Scot Class 4-6-0 No 6116 *Irish Guardsman*. National Railway Museum

given 70 years of faultless service, during which it was estimated to have travelled well over one-million miles. What could be a better compliment to its designer and the works that built it?

In 1922 the LNWR merged with the Lancashire & Yorkshire Railway and that company's engineering chief, George Hughes, became CME of the newly combined railway firm. However, Mr Beames stayed on at the works and served under Hughes with the title of Mechanical Engineer Crewe until his retirement in 1934..

Notably Whale presided over the production the Precursor Class of 4-4-0 twin-inside cylinder express passenger engines, the first of which emerged from Crewe some nine months after he took charge. After

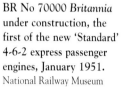

BR No 70000 *Britannia* under construction, the first of the new 'Standard' 4-6-2 express passenger engines, January 1951.
National Railway Museum

the class had been proven in service, he went on to produce a 4-6-0 express locomotive called the Experiment Class.

In 1906 George Whale unveiled the first of his successful 19in goods locomotives, a class also referred to as Experiment Goods. He later on in the same year introduced a 6ft four-coupled side-tank intended for suburban work on the lines in and around London, Birmingham and Manchester. Whale retired in 1910 to be replaced by CJ Bowen-Cooke, again in July, a month proving popular for changes in management.

The first milestone to be passed under Bowen-Cooke's reign was the 5000th locomotive build. This was when a George V class 4-4-0, No 5000 and given

the name *Coronation,* left the works in June 1911.

The name of Bowen-Cooke is synonymous with the famous London North Western Railway 'Super D' class 0-8-0 superheated goods engine. In 1913 the CME presided over the introduction of the very successful Claughton class of 4-6-0 express passenger locomotives.

During the First World War, Crewe Works was heavily committed to the production of munitions and other pieces of equipment to aid the war effort. On 18 October 1920 Bowen-Cooke died in service and was replaced by HPM Beames on 1 November. In 1922 the LNWR merged with the Lancashire & Yorkshire Railway and that company's engineering chief, George Hughes, became CME of the new railway firm. Beames stayed on at the works and served under Hughes with the title mechanical engineer Crewe until his retirement in 1934.

The following year was the year of the railway groupings brought about after the First World War as many of the UK's smaller railway companies were near to bankruptcy. As a result there were four large companies formed and they were the London Midland and Scottish Railway, London and North Eastern Railway, Great Western Railway and the Southern Railway. The grouping was decreed by the 1921 Railways Act passed on 19 August that year and made law on 1 January 1923. The LNWR was thus absorbed by the LMS.

The LMS introduced the Patriot class of 52 engines, the first two of which were rebuilds of Nos 5902 and 5971 from the famous LNWR Claughton class of locomotives. They became Nos 5500 *Patriot* and 5501 *St Dunstans.* The remaining 50 were officially considered rebuilds, although the parallel-boilered three-cylinder express passenger locomotives had very little of the Claughton engines in them.

In 1932 the LMS appointed William Arthur Stanier their CME and that marked the beginning of what many refer to as the 'Golden Age' of steam locomotive building at Crewe. In June 1933 the first of Stanier's Pacifics emerged from the works in the shape of 4-6-2 No 6200 *The Princess Royal.*

Just before the introduction of the Princess Royal class, Stanier's successful moguls were introduced, a Crewe build totalling 40 engines. Both classes featured boilers that were used for the first time by the LMS and became known as the 'Stanier tapered boiler'.

The first Stanier 'Black Five' 4-6-0s to emerge from Crewe Works rolled out in 1935, but examples of the design had earlier been built by the Vulcan Foundry in 1934. June 1937 saw the exciting introduction of Stanier's world-famous Princess Coronation class of Pacifics, the first 10 of which, and a later batch of 14, were streamlined, the total number built being 38.

In all, Stanier introduced to the LMS 11 classes of engine between 1933 and 1943, also including the Jubilee 4-6-0; 2-6-2 and 2-6-4 tank locomotives; and the very successful 8F 2-8-0 freight locomotives. He instigated the conversion of 70 Royal Scot 4-6-0s in 1943, which were originally a 1927 Fowler design for the LMS. Stanier retired as CME to the LMS in 1944, having been knighted for his services to the railway industry a year earlier.

A man who had the good fortune to be on the footplate of No 6220 *Coronation* when it set up a then-world speed record for steam (114mph) was an engineer who served at Crewe and who was destined to have his name linked with the so-called 'Standard' period of steam locomotive building.

He was Robert Arthur Riddles, who had joined the apprentice training school at Crewe in 1909 and went on to serve under Stanier before being appointed to

The 4-6-0 Jubilee class, designed by William A Stanier, was built at Crewe, Derby and the works of North British Locomotive Co (NBL). Pictured at 'The Works' in 2005 is a Crewe-built example, the preserved locomotive No 5690 *Leander,* which was outshopped in March 1936.
Author

The High Speed Train (HST). All the 193 power cars were built at Crewe and the first entered service in 1976. The extremely successful design is still in service with several Train Operating Companies (TOCs) in 2006, almost 40 years later. Author

the post of chief mechanical and electrical engineer for the newly formed British Railways in 1948. Incidentally, during the Second World War the bombers of a certain Mr A Hitler never managed to land any of their munitions on the main Crewe site. Following the war the four main railway companies in Britain were merged to form British Railways. That company was later marketed as British Rail.

In September 1950 the 7000th locomotive to be built at Crewe Works was listed as being an Ivatt Class 2MT 2-6-2 tank No 41272, which carried a commemorative plaque. The designer of the class, HG Ivatt, was another colleague of Stanier, and among the senior positions he held was that of principal assistant to the great man.

Quickly following the 7000th loco out of Crewe Works was the eagerly awaited first representative of a new class that carried the number 70000 and was called *Britannia*. That 4-6-2 express passenger engine emerged from the works in January 1951 and was the first from a class that numbered 55 locomotives,

all built at Crewe. A smaller version of the Britannia class primarily intended for use in Scotland and the Borders was also produced at Crewe in 1951-52. Numbered 72000 to 72009, the class 6 4-6-2s were known as Clans.

In 1954 a development of the Britannia class numbered 71000 and named *Duke of Gloucester* was built at Crewe. It was to be the only member of the class and was of a revolutionary design. In December of the same year, the first British Railways-built 9F 2-10-0 No 92000 was completed. This class of powerful freight engines has been described as the most successful of the Standards, and 251 were built between the works at Crewe and Swindon over a period of four years.

In December 1958 a member of the 9F 2-10-0 class had the distinction of being the last steam locomotive to be built at the works and, carrying No 92250, it was claimed to be the 7331st engine built at Crewe. However, historians have since recalculated that, in reality, it was more likely to have been the 7357th Crewe-built engine.

Class 87 AC Electric locomotive built in 1974 for use after the West Coast Main Line electrification was completed. Author

Crewe Locomotive Works thereafter became a centre for engineering and the production of diesel and electric locomotives, initially while still under the British Railways banner. Significantly it carried out the last steam engine repair for the nationalised company when Britannia class No 70013 *Oliver Cromwell* left the facility after repairs on 2 February 1967.

The company name was changed to British Rail Engineering – in 1988 it became BREL 1988 Ltd. In 1989 the company became ABB Ltd (Asea Brown Boveri) after privatisation. There followed a period under the ownership of Daimler Chrysler Rail Systems, branded Adtranz Ltd. Bombardier acquired Adtranz in May 2001 and the company then became part of the transportation group owned by the French Canadian company and worldwide conglomerate.

In 2005 the owners carried out an in-depth review of the site, after which it was said that several options, including expansion, rationalisation and closure, were considered. There were also substantive reports of a management buyout proposal. In September of that year a group of senior Crewe managers approached Bombardier with a view to taking over 'The Works' and operating it as a stand-alone railway engineering company, having prepared a comprehensive business plan.

During the period surrounding The Great Gathering (8-13 September), there were very strong rumours circulating that the MBO was to be accepted. Indeed, members of the Press were put on notice to expect an announcement to that effect during the GG event.

However, the proposed purchase was turned down as the Bombardier directors decided to pursue alternative options.

Recommended reading are two important and substantive works entitled respectively *A Pictorial Tribute to Crewe Works, In the Age of Steam* and *An Illustrated History of LNWR Engines* by Edward Talbot. Both are published by Oxford Publishing Co.

Diesel locomotive servicing at Crewe in the 1960s.
National Railway Museum

Webb 0-6-2T Coal Tank
locomotive No 1054. Built at
Crewe by the LNWR in 1888.
Pictured at Ingrow on the
Keighley & Worth Valley Railway.
Brian Sharpe

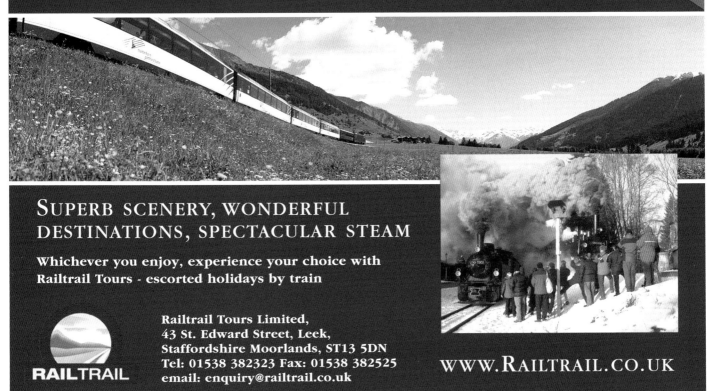

Keeping the PAST ALIVE!

Following the withdrawal of steam traction by British Railways, there was a hurried, and in some ways ad hoc scramble to save a varied selection of steam engines from the cutter's torch.

In total and excluding the large number of industrial locomotives, there are 432 standard gauge steam locomotives listed as preserved in the UK, and six replica engines. Of that number there still exist many that have yet to turn a wheel in preservation and therefore have effectively been under restoration for 40 years or more.

'Jinty' No 47445 pictured at Crewe in 1963. This is one of 10 examples of these tank locos that are preserved. They were a Midland design perpetuated by LMS. This example was built by the Hunslet Engine Co of Leeds in 1927. Mike Stokes Archive

Note. *A railway's gauge is the measurement (width) between the inner faces of the railway metals on a straight length of track. That was traditionally 4ft 8½in (1435mm) but in modern times, and mainly because a tighter fit between wheel and rail is said to give greater stability, much of the UK network has been reduced to a gauge of 4ft 8⅛in.*

No 80072, a Standard Class 4 2-6-4 tank locomotive being rebuilt, is owned by a group at the Llangollen Railway. It makes a fine sight in an erecting shop at Crewe Works during the 2005 Great Gathering. Author

Made in Crewe

Crewe-built locomotives back in 'The Works' for the 2005 Great Gathering. Front to rear 2-6-0 2MT No 46441 built by BR in 1950; 2-6-0 5MT No 2968 built by LMS in 1934; 4-6-0 5XP No 5690 *Leander* built by LMS in 1936. Author

Locomotives from a selection of types operated by all four 'Grouping' companies — LMS, LNER, GWR and SR — have been 'saved' but the railway that has more of its types preserved (including the 19 built under BR rule) is the Great Western Railway with 136 survivors. As far as examples of locomotive 'types' preserved are concerned, several classes stand out for recognition because of the number saved.

Those in double figures include 20 ex-SR West Country/Battle of Britain 4-6-2s (six built by BR), 18 ex-London Midland Scottish 'Black Five' 4-6-0s, 16 Great Western Railway Hall Class (although five of those were built under BR rule), and 15 4MT 2-6-4 BR Standard 4 tank locomotives. There are also16 ex-GWR pannier tanks of the 57xx 0-6-0PT type (two built under BR) and 14 examples of the ex-GWR 45xx 2-6-2T, plus 10 ex-LMS 'Jinty' 0-6-0T tank engines.

There are 108 active preserved railways in the UK and, of that total, some 29 operate on narrow gauge tracks. In addition there are 30 museums that have predominantly railway exhibits and at least 15 miniature railways. There are seven operational preserved railways on the island of Ireland.

Almost all the heritage railways have steam locomotives as their centrepiece but a great many also have departments dedicated to diesel and multiple unit preservation. The West Somerset Railway has the highest listed individual route mileage at 20 and, in total, there are almost 500 route miles of track in the UK.

The number of listed Crewe-built preserved examples is 40 locomotives, and that figure includes ex-London & North Western Railway-built machines. In addition to several at the National Railway Museum, the Crewe survivors are spread around the preserved network and many are main line certificated.

During the 1960s the railway authorities had already agreed to sell into preservation specific examples. Therefore before the 13 August 1968 steam deadline was in place, some locomotives moved directly from BR revenue-earning service into private ownership. One such engine was the much-loved Crewe icon, Stanier 4-6-2 Pacific No 6201 *Princess Elizabeth*.

PRINCESS ROYAL CLASS 4-6-2

Power classification	7P (later revised 8P)
Built	Crewe between 1933 and 1935, 13 locomotives built, all named, LMS number sequence 6200-6212 (46200-46212)
Designer	Sir WA Stanier for the London Midland and Scottish Railway.

No 46203 *Princess Margaret Rose* heading for Chester and the north Wales coast in 1996. Author

No 46200 *The Princess Royal*. The locomotive is seen out of service and in store at Carlisle Upperby (12A) in 1960. Note the name plates have been removed. Mike Stokes Archive

The appearance of No 6200 *The Princess Royal* in June 1933 heralded a new high-speed era for the LMS and its services on the West Coast Main Line. Stanier was set the task of developing a loco with enough capacity to complete the entire London-Glasgow journey (401 miles) at speed, while hauling trains of 500 tons. His solution was the Princess Royal Class.

It is a widely held belief that, while designing this class, Stanier drew on the knowledge he had gained working for the Great Western Railway, with his inspiration being that company's successful four-cylinder King Class. When the first Princess Royal locomotive emerged from Crewe Works, it was seen to be a much bigger passenger engine than anything else operating at the time on the West Coast Main Line. The locomotive weighed in at 104 tons 10cwt with the tender adding another 56 tons 7cwt (total 160 tons 17cwt). This was over 30 tons heavier (combined weight) than the Royal Scot locos, some of whose WCML work roster they were intended to cover.

Though at first being thought to be 'shy' steamers, the Princess Royals proved to be popular locomotives and, after their initial problems, were proved to be well up to the task in hand. No 6201 *Princess Elizabeth* adequately proved the point when, on 16 November 1936, it covered the Euston-Glasgow journey in a record time of 5hr 53min 38sec while hauling a seven-coach train. During that impressive journey the engine recorded a remarkable average speed of 68.2mph.

That record was achieved by a very famous Crewe North driver, Tom Clarke, with his regular fireman Charles Fleet and relief fireman Albert Shaw. RA Riddles, who was principal assistant to Stanier, also travelled on the footplate. Driver Clarke always maintained that he could have gone a lot faster,

No 46203 *Princess Margaret Rose* is pictured near the main gate of 'The Works' in the week prior to The Great Gathering 2005. Author

Fireman Fleet and Driver Tom Clarke (with the tankard) are toasted by their colleagues at Euston after the record runs with No 6201. Clive Mojonnier Collection

Waiting to return to the Midland Railway Centre after The Great Gathering, No 46203 in 'The Works'. Author

but the rules laid down by EJH Lemon, operating vice-president of the LMS, who travelled with the train, prohibited a speedier run.

Thomas James Clarke, from Bedford Street, Crewe, was a traditional railwayman and typical of those who worked trains of all links from both Crewe running sheds North 5A and South 5B, during the steam era. On 12 July 1937 Tom drove the Royal Train from Crewe to Euston and, on arrival at Euston, he was sent for by King George VI and, in the presence of Princess Elizabeth (after whom No 6201 was named), he was awarded the Order of the British Empire. He then proudly became Driver Tom Clarke OBE in recognition of his driving skills with No 6201 during his record-breaking runs. Tom died on 4 February 1954 aged 80, having retired from the railway 15 years earlier. He was, without doubt, one of Crewe's finest.

Two members of the class have survived into preservation and fortunately No 6201 *Princess Elizabeth* is one of them, the other being No 46203 *Princess Margaret Rose,* which was built in 1935. *Princess Elizabeth* is currently mainline certificated, is owned and operated by the 6201 Princess Elizabeth Locomotive Society Ltd and is based at the East

Lancashire Railway. *Princess Margaret Rose* is based at the Midland Railway Centre, Butterley and is owned and operated by The Princess Royal Class Locomotive Trust.

Examples of the class preserved
No 6201 *Princess Elizabeth,* built 1933.
No 46203 *Princess Margaret Rose,* built 1935.

No 6201 receiving attention in the shops at Crewe Works. Rail Archive Stephenson/ W H Whitworth

Back home! No 6201 beneath the vaulted roof of Liverpool Lime Street station on 1 April 2006. Author

No 6201
Princess Elizabeth

The first new type of locomotives designed for the LMS by the legendary railway engineer William A Stanier for use on the express trains of the West Coast Main Line were the 4-6-2 type Class 8P Princess Royal tender engines, all built at Crewe between 1933 and 1935 (see separate item in this publication). The story of No 6201 is a good example of modern preservation and main line steam operations.

Locomotive No 6201 was outshopped from Crewe Works on 3 November 1933 as part of an initial order for three locomotives, as an element of an overall

class of 13 machines. Together with No 6200 *Princess Royal,* No 6201 was covered under LMS Lot No 99 and Order No 371. Interestingly, it was also referred to by the LMS by the maker's number, 107, which can be seen stamped on parts of the engine's link motion to this day.

'To this day' being the relevant phrase! Thanks to the combined efforts of a great many people, and what can be described in modern parlance as a 'shed full of cash', the sight of No 6201 *Princess Elizabeth* on the main line and in full cry can still be enjoyed some 73 years after it first left Crewe Works to begin

Posed for a Hornby Hobbies advert in 1937. Driver Tom Clark at Edge Hill admiring the new model. Were you one of those schoolboys?
Hornby/6201 Society

revenue-earning service from Camden Motive Power Department (1B). The locomotive is certified for main line running until November 2009.

Princess Elizabeth is, of course, only one of the great many steam locomotives in preservation, and they almost all rely on the efforts of volunteer workers and supporters for their continued existence. In particular, those locomotives that plan to operate on the national network need a dedicated support crew to sustain them. When preserved engines are operated by and at a preserved railway, that organisation will almost always be in partnership with an owner or owning group responsible for looking after the asset to a pre-determined plan.

Volunteers are the very lifeblood of the steam special business and, of course, the preserved railways. Each main line 'pretender' must, in addition, have a private coach for the 'crew' and their equipment, to accompany the locomotive as it moves around the national network.

When a preserved steam locomotive is rostered for use on the main line, there are many factors to be taken into account even before the first passenger takes his or her seat. Is the physical size and weight

of the locomotive compatible with the limitations of the route over which the planned journey is required to run? It may be that the infrastructure is now vastly different from the days when the particular locomotive type first (if ever) travelled the route.

The reasons for possible incompatibilities are too numerous to list here and they can vary from the alteration of a particular section of track layout to the raising of the height of the track bed or the alteration of a station platform. Applications to 'gauge' preserved locomotives for a special run are currently made to Network Rail by a tour operator in partnership with the locomotive owning body. The potential route must include places where the engine can take on water and even, on some of the longer runs, a stock of coal. Loading coal and watering the locomotive is almost always down to the support crew.

Railways are dangerous places and, accordingly, the members of support crews must by necessity be made up only of individuals who are in possession of a current PTS (Personal Track Safety) Certificate. Any special train must be fitted into the daily timetable for the route concerned without causing even the slightest disruption to normal services and, in some

Passing Rugby at speed with the Euston-Liverpool 'Merseyside Express' on 4 July 2003.
John Whitehouse/6201 Society

instances, it might be necessary to include in the route track sections where the 'special' can lodge in order to let a service train(s) pass.

The operator will then set about attempting to sell enough tickets to cover their overheads which will, of course, include the cost of track access, locomotive hire, rolling stock hire etc. In order to operate the locomotive a Train Operating Company (TOC) would be engaged to supply trained footplate crew. Indeed, some of the longer journeys could mean more than one crew being assigned. The 'hired-in' footplate staff would comprise a driver, fireman and traction inspector; on occasions there might be two firemen.

On board the train, in addition to the tour operator's people, the TOC (Train Operating Company) will supply a train manager who, to all intents and purposes, carries the responsibility for seeing that the 'special' fits seamlessly into the day's overall schedule. Their

tasks will also include the supervision of any shunting, fuelling, watering and, if necessary, turning of the locomotive in partnership with the train crew(s).

What follows are some details of an actual main line run with No 6201 *Princess Elizabeth,* heading a Birmingham-Liverpool return special in April 2006. The steam locomotive was to go on the stock (which had travelled north hauled by modern traction) at Bescot Depot, north of Birmingham on the West Coast Main Line. Steam traction is not permitted to enter Birmingham New Street station.

The steamer left its overnight stabling-point at the Railway Age, Crewe, at 6.30 on the morning of the run (April 1). The support crew had slept in their coach, having spent the previous two days preparing No 6201 for the round-trip journey. Many of the volunteer crew had unselfishly taken holidays from 'the day job' in order to be there.

Made in Crewe

A failure by the modern diesel locomotive bringing the special and its travellers from London meant that, although No 6201 was turned and facing north right on time, the 'steam special' would not depart until almost one-and-a-half hours later than scheduled. At least the delay allowed the crew to enjoy their fried breakfast-cum-lunch in peace. With the stock 'hooked on' and the steam crew given the road, the special departed for its first stop at Crewe.

The first problem was, of course, slotting the special into a new path in the busy WCML working timetable. That done successfully, the supervisor at Crewe station (in league with the duty signaller for that section) needed to make sure that the all-important Platform 12 was available at the new time, so that the engine could take water. The next hurdle was an unexpected one: the local water supply was experiencing a big drop in pressure!

From top:

A Princess should always look her best! Geoff Sharrock gets to work.

Nothing is left unchecked before a run. Left to right are: Colin Worrall, Roy Kerry (both on loco) and Steve Blackmoor.

Three members of the all-important No 6201 sales team, left to right: Ron Perry, Barbara Tooley and Jill Mojonnier.

The 'down' loco crew for the April 1 run. On the loco are driver Bob Morrison and fireman Pete Sheridan with traction inspector Bob Hart on the steps.

All author

The Queen is presented with a model of No 6201 by Clive Mojonnier at Crewe.
Pete Skelton/6201 Society

As No 6201 began taking on water, Roy Kerry, the owning trusts CME (Chief Mechanical Engineer), was anxiously looking at his flow meter and working out whether the operation could be completed in the time allowed. The crew, which included Locomotive 6201 Princess Elizabeth Society Ltd Chairman Clive Mojonnier, worked smartly. Watered sufficiently for the journey to Liverpool, the special continued bang on time.

On arrival at Lime Street, the passengers disembarked for a shortened visit to the soon-to-be City of Culture while the stock was pulled backwards in order to free up the platform and gain access to a now mainly disused part of railway infrastructure adjacent to the WCML. The locomotive then went 'light' to turn at Earlestown before rejoining the support coach in order to be serviced.

That entailed watering the engine again, this time from a hydrant in a street some 250 yards away from the running line on which No 6201 was parked. Then vehicle access to the secure site had to be arranged (in practical terms, finding the Network Rail guy with the key to the gate) so that a tipper wagon with five tons of steam coal could be brought alongside the engine.

Fortunately the wagon had a hydraulic grab with which to load the coal but, even so, members of the support crew had to climb on top to settle the load. This area is 'safe' as it does not have any overhead electric wires.

While this was taking place locomotive crews were changed over pending the return journey, and the normal service checks and oiling took place. There are no passengers on support crews and every member of the No 6201 team had specific and very necessary tasks to perform, not least of was the catering manager, whose efforts were greatly appreciated. Not only was hot tea plentiful but a very appetising meal of stew and dumplings was being prepared for all to

enjoy once the locomotive was back on the stock and the passengers settle into their seats.

The locomotive then went on to work the special back to Bescot (with a water stop at Crewe), where the diesel took over again. Turned and serviced, *Princess Elizabeth* and its support coach then returned to its home base at the East Lancashire Railway.

Even with changes and a degree of shift working, the volunteer support crews of steam specials still unselfishly work long hours in order to contribute to the enjoyment of many.

So fragile are the costing structures of special trains and, indeed, preservation in general, that, if the countless volunteers were to be replaced by paid staff, it is doubtful if such operations could break even, let alone make a profit. In the case of the owners, they need enough income to refurbish their charges approximately every 10 years. Such costs are truly astronomical.

From top:

Hot work for Colin Worrall as he gets to work on the fire between runs.

(Steady) Eddie Williamson, the driver for the return leg, checks over No 6201 prior to backing on the train.

Supercook No 6201 catering guru Richard Raynor – some say the most important man on the train.

The proof as they say... Clive Mojonnier gets to work on the beef stew and dumplings 6201-style.

All author

Together with possible increasing track access charges and now the need to fit the main line preserved locomotives with OTMR (On Train Monitoring and Recording) equipment, referred to as 'black box recorders', the costs are set to rise.

In 2009 when No 6201 is due to be examined with a view to receiving the work necessary to obtain a new boiler certificate (a legal requirement before any steamings can take place), the cost is,

say the locomotive's management team, likely to be in the region of £250,000. When the engine came back to the main line in 2002 a conservative estimate put the overall total expenditure on No 6201 at around £400,000.

Many who are well-versed in the ways of preservation openly say that hire fees alone are increasingly unlikely to cover the cost of operating and maintaining steam locomotives. There are National Lottery grants to be applied for, but that

source has many other calls on its funds.

Thus the efforts of those ladies and gentlemen with the sales trolleys on the trains, and with stands at railway events, are crucially important. The '6201' team are especially well-blessed in that regard and Jill Mojonnier and her enthusiastic band are to be congratulated on their efforts. Locomotive and preserved railway sales teams are as equally important in keeping the restored wheels turning as are the volunteer engineers and support crews.

An excellent publication by 6201 group chairman Clive Mojonnier detailing fully the history and rescue of the engine is available from the 6201 Princess Elizabeth Society Ltd.
***6201 Princess Elizabeth* is priced at £14 inc p&p.**
Details from PO Box No 6201, Millom,
Cumbria LA18 4GE or by email to
Sales@steamrailwaynews.org.uk

Ais Gill summit on the Settle & Carlisle line is topped by 6201 in great style.
John Leck/6201 Society

6201 *a brief history*

1933 November 3:	Outshopped from Crewe Works
1933 November 4:	Commenced working Euston-Glasgow express services.
1935-38:	Regularly worked both the up and down 'Royal Scot' trains.
1936 November 16:	The first of two record-breaking runs for the LMS.
1936 November 17:	The second of two record-breaking runs for the LMS.
1939 August 11:	Recorded for the first time working the down 'Merseyside Express' London-Liverpool.
1949-1960:	Continued to work express and named trains on the WCML including, 'The Red Rose', 'Midday Scot', 'The Royal Scot' and the 'Merseyside Express'.
1961 March 6:	Taken out of service and put into store at Carlisle.
1961 May:	Taken out of store and put back to work.
1961 October:	Placed in store again. Fund started to preserve the locomotive.
1962 January 26:	Taken out of store again and put back to work.
1962 September 10:	Put into store at Carlisle Kingmoor for the final time.
1962 October 20:	Officially withdrawn from traffic by British Railways.
1963:	The locomotive is bought for preservation at a cost of £2160-00
1976 April 24:	First main line run in preservation deputising for GWR loco No 6000 *King George V,* Hereford-Newport-Hereford.
1976 June 5:	Hauled WA Stanier Centenary Special between Hereford and Chester.
1979 May:	Participated in the Rocket 150 celebrations at Rainhill.
1980 July 4:	Returned with a special train to Carlisle, after 17 years!
1983:	The locomotive is stood down from main line work in order to allow a complete refurbishment.
1986 November 15:	Returned to the main line.
1987 July 24:	The locomotive is visited by the Queen, who is presented with a model of the engine.
1994 November:	The engine is taken out of service to allow another seven-year boiler examination etc to take place.
2002 April 29:	Running in after the rebuild began on the East Lancashire Railway.
To August 2006:	No 6201 *Princess Elizabeth* is still appearing regularly on the main line and is also often seen running over the preserved metals of her home base the East Lancashire Railway.

Made in Crewe

No 6201 on the
Settle & Carlisle route.
John Cooper-Smith/6201 Society

Over the weekend of 10-11 September the Webb Crewe Works Charity Fund staged the Great Gathering — Festival of Rail Open Weekend.

Among the visiting locomotives were products of other locomotive works loaned for the occasion by the participating preserved railways. These two fine examples are from the Llangollen Railway.

Jessie 0-6-0 saddle tank works No 1873, built 1937 Hunslet Engine Co Leeds, rests overnight on the Friday prior to the event.

No 7822 *Foxcote Manor* 4-6-0, built 1950 to a GWR design by British Railways is seen having newly arrived at the works in the week prior to the event. Both Author

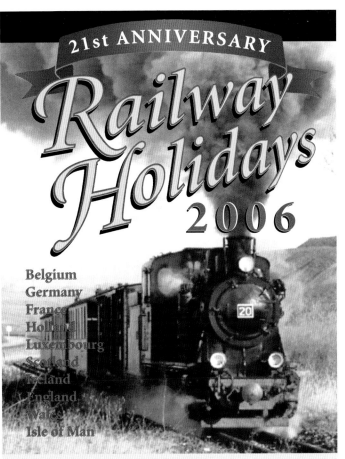
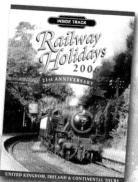

PRINCESS CORONATION CLASS 4-6-2

Power classification	7P (later revised 8P)
Built	Crewe between 1937 and 1948, 38 locomotives built and all named. LMS number sequence 6220-6257 (46220-46257)
Designer	Sir WA Stanier for the London Midland and Scottish Railway.

No 46229 *Duchess of Hamilton* seen on the 'North Wales Coast Express' at Abergele in July 1991.
Author

No 46228 *City of Carlisle* seen passing under Kilburn High Road in June 1964.
Mike Stokes Archive

In 1935 the London & North Eastern Railway (LNER) introduced a batch of streamlined class A4 locomotives to operate on its prestigious high-speed London-to-Scotland services along the East Coast Main Line. In answer to this challenge, the LMS reacted by building the Princess Coronation class of four-cylinder Pacifics with which to operate its Anglo-Scottish services.

The first five of these engines, numbered 6220-6224, were streamlined with what was described by many observers at the time as a 'bathtub' shroud shape of steel air-smooth casing.

They were painted in a distinctive blue and silver chevron-striped livery. A further five streamlined locomotives were outshopped from Crewe in the following year, numbered 6225-6229, and they were also adorned with the chevron stripes. However, they were finished in a maroon-and-gilt colour scheme and the LMS publicity stated that they, too, would work Scottish expresses but additionally London-Liverpool trains.

The locomotives, together with their distinctive trains, were a huge success with the travelling public and, in addition to being extremely powerful engines, were sure-footed machines and very fast movers. Cashing in on this success, the LMS sent a complete train to tour the USA in 1938 in order to be exhibited at the World's Fair, after which it visited 38 cities and covered 3120 miles on American rails. The doyen of the class, No 6220 *Coronation,* was not made available for the tour so the later-built No 6229 *Duchess of Hamilton* temporarily assumed the identity of the record-holder and was duly sent to the USA.

The remaining members of the class were delivered to the LMS between 1939 and 1943, and locomotives Nos 6230-6234 were built without air-smooth casing; however, the next batch, Nos 6235-6248, were built as streamliners. The next group of seven locos to

Smoke galore as No 6233 blasts through Selside (S&C) on a Royal Train conveying Prince Charles in March 2005. David Jones

No 46246 *City of Manchester* at Beattock Summit with the 'up' 'Mid-Day Scot' in August 1958. Note the slope on the top of the smoke box, denoting an ex-streamlined locomotive. David Anderson

No 6229 as a 'semi' with the smoke box altered in anticipation of receiving a streamlined casing. Seen at Tyseley in May 2006. Brian Wilson

leave the works (Nos 6249-6255) were built without streamlining. The last two (Nos 6256/7) were also unstreamlined but built after Stanier's reign by his successor, HG Ivatt, who made modifications that included the fitting of roller bearings and a redesigned trailing truck.

During the four years 1945-1949, the streamlining was removed from all of the class, after which they appeared in five different liveries, lined black, lined green, two shades of blue and lined maroon. All of the engines in this popular class were withdrawn between 1962 and 1964 and three examples have been preserved. They include ex-streamliner No 46229 *Duchess of Hamilton,* which is owned by the nation, resides at the National Rail Museum, York, and is currently a non-runner. This much-travelled Princess Coronation class ex-LMS locomotive is now in the process of being returned to its 1938 streamlined appearance. The second surviving member of the class, No 46235 *City of Birmingham,* is firmly 'brick walled' into a display area at the Birmingham Museum of Science and Industry.

However, the profile of the class has been kept at the highest level by the post-millennium main line performances of sister loco No 6233 *Duchess of Sutherland,* resplendent in LMS maroon livery.

This engine is normally based at the Midland Railway Centre, Butterley, Derbyshire.

It is owned and operated by The Princess Royal Class Locomotive Trust and it has, at the time of writing, in addition to other regular tour work, hauled the Royal Train on two separate occasions.

Examples of the class preserved
No 6223 *Duchess of Sutherland*
No 46229 *Duchess of Hamilton*
No 46235 *City of Birmingham*

An LMS enthusiast's 'Dream Team': Nos 6233, 46229, 46203 and 6201. Pictured in 'The Works' in September 2005. Author

THE **Coronation Scot**

| EUSTON | DEPART 1.30 P.M. | GLASGOW (CENTRAL) DEPART 1.30 P.M. |
| GLASGOW (CENTRAL) ARRIVE 8.0 P.M. | | EUSTON ARRIVE 8.0 P.M. |

COMMENCING JULY 5TH (MONDAYS TO FRIDAYS)

6½ HOURS

LONDON MIDLAND & SCOTTISH RAILWAY

Made in Crewe

'Coronation Scot'

Introduced in 1937, the streamlined
'Coronation Scot' train was a 'total concept'
designed and built by the London Midland &
Scottish Railway in order to achieve fast travel
between London Euston and Glasgow Central. The
specially designed locomotives were built at Crewe
Works and the carriage sets at the Wolverton LMS
works.

On the lucrative and prestige routes from the
capital to the north, the rival London & North Eastern
Railway had effectively stolen a march on the
LMS by introducing their Gresley-designed
streamlined A4 locomotives on 'Silver Jubilee' trains
over the East Coast Main Line between London King's
Cross and Newcastle.

In fact the LNER had thrown down the gauntlet
when their celebrated A1 Pacific No 4472 *Flying
Scotsman* hauled the first train to reach an
authenticated 100mph on 30 November 1934. Two
years later one of the LNER's A4 Pacific streamlined
locomotives and its matching 'Silver Jubilee' train
broke that record by a full 12mph during a journey
on the ECML on 29 September 1935.

The new benchmark was thus set at 112mph and
that fact stirred the LMS in general, and their chief
engineer William A Stanier in particular, into

designing and building a train to win back the
cosseted blue ribbon. The successful outcome was
the 'Coronation Scot', comprising a streamlined
4-6-2 steam locomotive and a matching set of
nine coaches.

The locomotives, which were at first given a power
classification of 7P (P for passenger), were later
reclassified 8P by British Railways. They carried the
class name Princess Coronation and the 4-6-2 tender
locomotives were built between 1937 and 1948.
In total there were 38 members of the class built
and not all were streamlined (see separate item in
this publication).

In a 1937 article for the railway Press, the LMS
gave the following summation of the new
Coronation Scot concept: 'New 4-6-2 locomotives and
nine-coach trains for working the LMSR accelerated
six-and-a-half-hour express service between Euston
and Glasgow to commence on 5 July. The engines are
streamlined and, like the trains, are finished
throughout in blue and silver'.

The name 'Coronation Scot' was chosen in order
to commemorate the coronation of King George VI
(12 May 1937). The stylised named train ran from
July 1937 until the start of the Second World War
in 1939.

Official works picture of
No 6220 *Coronation*.
National Railway Museum

That original announcement of the new west coast express service concerned only five locomotives and three sets of matching rolling stock. The engines were:

> No 6220 *Coronation*
> No 6221 *Queen Elizabeth*
> No 6222 *Queen Mary*
> No 6223 *Princess Alice*
> No 6224 *Princess Alexandra*

The new locomotives reportedly cost the LMS £11,813 each to build.

The first 'Coronation Scot' train was presented to the Press at Crewe station following a lunch at the nearby Crewe Arms Hotel on Tuesday 26 May 1937, a full six weeks before the first planned main line run. The Press were said to have received the new rail travel concept well and they were very complimentary about it but, given the earlier LNER Silver Jubilee scheme, they probably had comparisons uppermost in their minds!

The Press party were welcomed to the launch by none other than WA Stanier, and the after-lunch inspection of the new train was conducted under the guidance of EA Lemon, who was the Crewe Works superintendent at the time.

Scrutinising a cross-section of their reports gives the overall impression that the newsmen were all mightily impressed by the new train in its own right, and few of the early reports made a direct comparison with the LNER trains — except, that was, to surmise on whether the LMS would win back the speed record.

The LMS design office made no secret of the fact that the new locomotives were inspired by, and a development of, the highly successful Princess Royal class of 4-6-2s built at Crewe between 1933 and 1935. In fact the *Railway Gazette* at the time reported that 'the possibility of high-speed running on the West Coast Main Line had been investigated (and proven) by speed trials held on the route on 16 and 17 November 1936'.

The locomotive involved in those trials was Princess Royal No 6201 *Princess Elizabeth* (see pages 32-41 in this publication).

The company reasoned that, apart from the obvious difference of the streamlined casing (which some commentators ungraciously called an inverted bath tub), the Princess Coronations had larger driving wheels, ie 6ft 9in in diameter

401½ (then) route miles between London and Glasgow had really taxing gradients for only between 30 and 40 of the total miles.

Therefore the emphasis on achieving and sustaining high speed on the level and easier graded sections of the route would pay off, as any loss in speed (or drop behind in timetabled schedule) on the graded sections would be more than compensated for by the gain of speed (and therefore the picking up of time) on the other sections. Hence the use of big driving wheels, which was established locomotive engineering practice for high-speed running.

The actual running time planned for the new service was 385 minutes and that timing included a five-minute stop at Carlisle. That schedule called for an average speed of 62.6mph to be achieved, a speed that meant both the locomotive and its crew must perform at, or at least near, the top limit of their capabilities.

The new nine-coach 'Coronation Scot' trains were to have a total weight of 297 tons. The normal configuration would provide 232 passenger seats, of which there would be 82 first class and 150 third class. Accordingly the meticulous locomotive engineers at Crewe left nothing to chance and the new class of locomotives was built with the precision more normally applied to a Swiss watch.

as opposed to 6ft 6in on the Princess Royals. Consider that design feature along with larger cylinders, a higher-capacity superheater and a larger grate area, and you begin to see that Stanier really meant business.

The intention of the design team was to produce a locomotive capable of sustained high-speed running and, in that regard, their thinking was that the

The 'Coronation Scot' one journey each way, Monday to Friday, including Euston, depart 1.30pm Glasgow arrive 8pm. Glasgow depart 1.30pm Euston arrive 8pm.
National Railway Museum

Front end view showing
four cylinders, steam chests
and upper framing.
Richard Metcalf Collection

Great attention was paid to the lubrication system in order that all moving parts operated freely.
The all-important routing of steam from the boiler to the four of 16½in by 28in cylinders was carefully engineered so as to allow free passage at all times. The exhaust steam and gases were dealt with in a similarly efficient manner.

The Princess Coronation class boiler was of normal LMS construction and the shell was made from high quality nickel steel with the firebox copper lined. The working pressure of the boiler was set at 250psi and, in that regard, was the same as the earlier Princess Royal engines.

The all-important firebox stays were mostly steel except for the outer ones and a top few rows, which were made of Monel* metal, as were the throat plate stays. The firebox was designed to extend into the boiler barrel in order to form a combustion chamber and thus allow the gases to complete their combustion before entering tubes (thereby heating the water surrounded them and turning it to steam). In short, no design innovation was left untried in order to build what Stanier promised would be an exceptional and very powerful class of steam locomotive.

Just a few of the facts appertaining to the locomotive's specification might help the modern reader understand and appreciate the capabilities of the Crewe workforce some 70 years ago. The main frames of the streamlined (or air-cooled casing fitted engines) were constructed of high tensile steel plate at a thickness of 1⅛in (2.85cm).

Boiler ready for
mounting on the frames.
Richard Metcalf Collection

*Monel (or monel metal) is a trademarked name for a range of corrosion-resistant bright metal alloys containing typically
67 per cent nickel, 30 per cent copper and trace proportions of iron, manganese and other elements.

Masquerading as sister locomotive No 6229 *Duchess of Hamilton* (whilst that locomotive was playing 'her' part in the USA) the first of the class No 6220 *Coronation* is pictured on the 'Coronation Scot'.
National Railway Museum

The streamlined locomotive including the tender was 73ft 9½in (22.48m) long outside the buffers and the chimney towered 13ft 2⅝in (4.04m) above the track. The weights in working order were locomotive and tender 164 tons 9 cwt (167.55 tonnes), tender only 56 ton 7cwt (57.61 tonnes).

The coal-carrying capacity was 10 tons (10.160 tonnes) and the water-carrying capacity 4000 gallons (18,184.36 litres). In order to assist the fireman, the tender was fitted with a steam-powered coal pusher that could be used to bring the coal forward as the stock was depleted during a journey.

The coupling and connecting rods (which connect together the main wheels and thus drive the loco by causing the wheels to turn) were made out of a special strong steel alloy called Vibrac, the like of which is used in modern times in the manufacture of high-pressure gas cylinders. As stated previously the diameter of the driving wheels was 6ft 9in (2.06m)

with the front bogie wheels at 3ft (0.914m), the trailing bogie wheels 3ft 9in (1.14 m) and the tender wheels 4ft 3in (1.29m).

The construction of the special coaches in many ways followed LMSR standard practice. The body sides, ends and roof were covered in steel panels finishing flush with the windows. The exterior painting of the initial streamliners was in Caledonian blue with four bands of silver running the full length of the train between the windows of the carriages and continuing alongside the engine to finish in a V-shaped point on the front of the smokebox.

The car numbers and lettering were in plain block silver characters, and exterior fittings such as door handles were finished in bright chromium plate. The cars were built on steel under frames and all, with the exception of the kitchen cars, were fitted with pressure heating and ventilation.

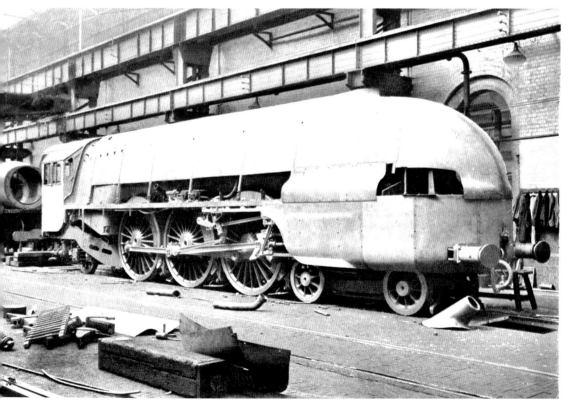

In the Crewe erecting shop the first engine being built, partly streamlined, the frames and smoke box of the second engine can be seen behind.
Richard Metcalf Collection

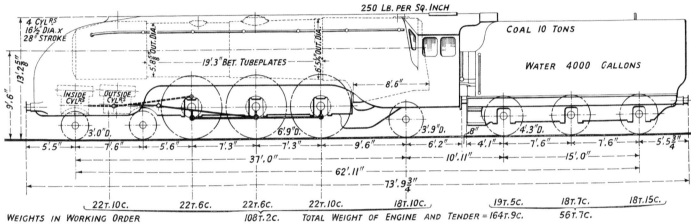

General view of
new locomotive and
outline diagram.
Richard Metcalf Collection

The normal nine-coach train configuration was an 18-seat Corridor First Brake, a 22-seat Corridor First, a 42-seat Vestibule First Diner, a Kitchen Car, 42-seat Vestibule 3rd, a 42-seat Vestibule 3rd Diner, a Kitchen Car, 42-seat Vestibule 3rd (Diner) and a Corridor Third Brake.

The coach interiors were finished in what for the age was a very modern style, and lighting was plentiful and imaginatively installed. The three initial coach sets were finished in different types of wood and each in its own way was said to be very attractive, and even described by some observers as futuristic.

To achieve the individual effects different timbers were used in every coach and all the panelling was fitted flush in order to give an impression of space. The first class vestibule cars varied from train to train. The furnishing and trimmings were alternatively in blue, green or brown and each set was completed in a different colour. The carpets were Wilton in both the first class corridor and vestibule cars and the 3rd class vestibule cars, with mostly heavy-duty cork floor coverings in the other units.

One first class dining car was finished in rich satin wood with Claro walnut doors, another train's

similar car was finished in Canadian mountain maple and the doors finished in Nigerian kevazingo, but in the third such car the style was less striking with the whole saloon being finished in English olive ash, though both straight and curly grain patterns were used.

The interiors of the third class vestibule cars in each set were also differently finished. The main timber and veneers used were English weathered sycamore, English burr sycamore, English curly oak butt with tiger stripe and Canadian silver elm. Interestingly the Canadian elm veneer came from timber recovered from Waterloo Bridge (built 1817) in London, which was pulled down in 1936. The wooden baulks had been under water for 119 years but were amazingly in a usable condition.

But what of that attempt to wrestle back the speed record from the LNER? The LMSR put on a special run for the benefit of the Press and invited dignitaries, and that took place on 29 June 1937. The new train hauled by No 6220 *Coronation* ran a return trip between London Euston and Crewe.

In charge of the 'down run' was the legendary Crewe steam footplateman Driver TJ Clarke and his fireman for the run C Lewis. Also on the engine were LMS engineer Robert Riddles (later of Standard

At speed on the WCML are No 6221 *Queen Elizabeth* and the 'Coronation Scot'.
National Railway Museum

Inset above: Interior of a 3rd class corridor compartment.
Richard Metcalf Collection

locomotive fame) and Inspector S Miller. The journey took place under normal working conditions and the inspector was no doubt there to see that, among other things, all speed restrictions were observed.

The journey of 158.1 miles (254.44km) called for the distance to be covered in 135 minutes averaging a speed of 70.2mph. Driver Clarke brought the train north in what some observers described as adequate but unspectacular fashion, no doubt due to the traffic and permanent way conditions he encountered en route. The train was, however, able to accelerate over the last section of its journey, and it was no secret that the LMS were after the record.

The railway line between Norton Bridge and Crewe had been specially prepared and aligned, allowing the previous maximum speed limit of 90 mph to be removed. From Norton Bridge the locomotive accelerated from a 60mph restriction as fast as it could, and in fact then topped 85mph at Whitmore with the speed still increasing rapidly. But the station at Crewe, with its multiplicity of cross-overs and points, was coming up fast, so the train was braked hard!

It braked so hard, in fact, that some said it was a miracle it stayed upright as it hurtled towards the entry to Crewe station's platform three, which entailed negotiating its three cross-overs.

General arrangement view of cab of No 6220 when new.
Richard Metcalf Collection

Reportedly, after that lively manoeuvre a very large amount of crockery in the dining cars needed replacing! Otherwise, thanks to the overall cleverness of the locomotive's design in general, and in particular its leading bogie arrangement, no more damage was done.

The LMSR claimed that a speed recorder on the engine had peaked at 114mph (183.46kph) and they produced a chart taken from the machine to substantiate the claim. Independent timing experts on the train who included the illustrious railway experts OS Nock and Cecil J Allen did not agree, stating that their top recorded speed for the run was 112.5mph (181.05kph)

The overall time was 129.75 minutes at a credible average 73.1mph; however, the last 1.1 miles into Crewe were achieved in a time of 1min 19sec. The cost in crockery was not recorded!

On the return 'up trip' to London the train had to observe speed restrictions of 30mph at Stafford and 40mph at Rugby, but nevertheless turned in a start-to-stop journey time of 119 minutes, averaging 79.9mph. Over the section from Walton to Willesden Junction, a distance of 69.9 miles, the train travelled for a period at the magic 100mph, and thus on that section averaged 89.3mph.

By comparison, the 2006 Virgin Pendelino timetable, with two scheduled stops at either Stafford, Nuneaton, Rugby or Watford Junction,

1937

No 6220 *Coronation*,
LMS publicity picture.
Crewe Works Archive

advertises Crewe-London journey times of between 112 and 115 minutes.

Following the two runs, the LMS claimed the fastest start-to-stop trains record over distances of 100 and 150 miles. But the LNER record of 112mph (180kph) remained intact in many people's opinions, mainly because the other timing experts were unable to confirm the 'Coronation Scot' speeds. The LMS widely made it known that, in its view, it at least shared the LNER record speed. That was, of course, until the events of 3 July 1938, which involved a certain LNER engine called *Mallard*.

The 'Coronation Scot' was also celebrated in music by way of a rousing piece of that name written by the composer Vivian Ellis. The music, which has since been used for other themes by the BBC, was originally used as the signature tune for the *Paul Temple private detective* radio programmes created by Francis Durbridge, and first broadcast in 1938.

Make-believe sleuth Temple and his wife, Steve, who was supposedly a glamorous Fleet Street journalist, entertained radio audiences for more than 30 years, thereby keeping the 'Coronation Scot' alive, at least in music, long after it had ceased to run.

Mr Ellis always maintained that his inspiration for the composition was, in fact, the express trains of the GWR (Great Western Railway), but the piece was named after the LMS train by his publisher. In a further act of confusion, the sheet music for a 1948 piano version of the tune was adorned with a picture of the LNER 'Silver Jubilee' train!

A complete 'Coronation Scot' train, described at the time by the LMS as 'luxurious', was shipped to the USA for exhibition in 1939.

For operational reasons, No 6220 *Coronation* was unable to make the trip so the newly constructed No 6229 *Duchess of Hamilton,* the 10th in the class, was sent with the carriages, but in the guise of *Coronation*. While in America the locomotive was driven during most of its steamings by the LMSR's RA Riddles.

The outbreak of World War II meant that the 1938 built No 6229, a 'red' engine, did not return to the UK until 1942! Interestingly No 6229's role as a red 'Coronation' (with a matching set of carriages) meant that for the duration of the American trip there was a blue Duchess of Hamilton running on British metals and a red Coronation running on American ones.

1956

No 46220 *Coronation* is pictured on a local stopping train between Edinburgh Princes Street and Glasgow Central, passing Balerno Junction. David Anderson

Visitors to *the Works*

Over the weekend of 10-11 September 2005 the Webb Crewe Works Charity Fund staged the Great Gathering – Festival of Rail Open Weekend. Among the visiting locomotives were products of other locomotive works loaned for the occasion by the participating preserved railways.

Class 28 Co-Bo No D5705 built in 1958 by Metropolitan Vickers is pictured receiving attention to its bogies whilst at the works. This loco is based at the East Lancashire Railway.

Class 27 Co-Co No 27000 ex Woodhead route DC electric built in 1953 at Gorton Works. This loco is based at the Midland Railway – Butterley.
Both Author

Made in Crewe

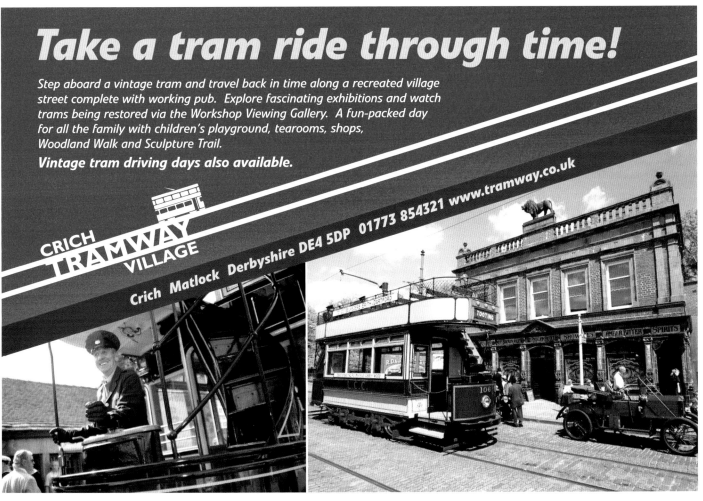

Crewe-built steam locomotive types

LNWR 'Super D' 0-8-0

Power classification	6F and 7F
Built	Various types built between 1910 and 1922 and also G2a rebuilds between 1936 and 1947 at Crewe Works. Total taken into BR ownership in 1948 – 478 locos made up of 98 G1 6F Class, 60 G2 7F Class and 320 G2a 7F Class.
Designer	Designed by Charles J Bowen-Cooke

Hard at work. The preserved 'Super D' 0-8-0 No 49395 is pictured at Consal Forge on the Churnet Valley Railway in 2005. David Gibson

No 49421, a G2 type in BR ownership, seen at Gorton MPD in March 1961. Mike Stokes Archive

Charles Bowen-Cooke (1859-1920) was the son of a church minister, like Francis William Webb, an earlier LNWR CME. He succeeded George Whale at Crewe on 1 July 1909. He was employed in the post for just over 11 years until his untimely death in service on 18 October 1920. In the preceding year, he served the town of Crewe as its mayor.

The 'Super D' was by no means his only contribution to LNWR locomotive development but it is the design for which he is most remembered. These impressive goods engines underwent various rebuilds and evolved into three distinct sub-classes, but all were known by railwaymen as 'Super Ds', a title worthy of explanation.

The term originally referred to a class of 62 engines that were, in fact, rebuilds from an earlier Francis W Webb three-cylinder design but had larger boilers. Between 1923 and 1927 these locomotives were rebuilt, becoming the G1 type. At that period in time, locomen had become used to calling every 0-8-0 engine with a large boiler a 'D'. After 1912, the practice of using superheating in boiler design gave rise to the term 'Super', hence these large-boilered 0-8-0s all became known as 'Super Ds'.

Steam created in the boiler at a specified pressure and temperature is known as saturated steam, as it is in contact with the water. Basically the superheating principle involves passing the saturated steam through a series of heater elements situated in the boiler's large flue tubes. The resultant steam when fed to the cylinders is hotter, drier and, as a result, has greater expansive qualities, thus producing more power.

The 'Super D' earned the reputation of being a very vocal locomotive and they could be heard miles away with their 'two-loud-then-two-gentle' exhaust beats, with the second of the loud beats noticeably louder than the first. In addition, the distinctive wheeze attributed to the type of Joy valve gear used on these engines, in conjunction with the constant ringing of

In LMS guise during 1946, No 9386, a 'Super D' G2a type at Heaton Mersey depot.
Mike Stokes Archive

An unidentified 'Super D' with an empty coaching stock train entering Manchester Victoria station in 1957. Manchester Exchange station is seen in the background.
Mike Stokes Archive

the side rods, reportedly made them audibly unique, even when they were not working flat-out.

The combined class gave great service and, although withdrawal from traffic started in 1947, several engines earned a reprieve and were, in fact, given heavy overhauls owing to a shortage of freight engines in the period immediately after the Second World War. The last five to work were still allocated to the engine sheds at Bescot (21B) and Bushbury (21C) in 1964.

Examples of the class preserved
No 49395 G2, built in 1921.

Preserved LNWR 'Super D' pictured after the completion of its rebuild by L&NWR Heritage Company Ltd, Crewe, 8 June 2005. Author

STANDARD CLASS 7 BRITANNIA 4-6-2

Power classification	(Mixed traffic) 7P6F
Built	1951-1954, 55 built. BR numbers allocated 70000-70054.
Designer	BR Standard locomotive by a team led by RA Riddles at BR Derby.

No 70000 *Britannia* with a steam special at Crewe in 1990. Brian Sharpe

No 70003 *John Bunyan* in filthy condition waits to back on to a train in Perth station, July 1964. Mike Stokes Archive

mmediately on being formed, the BR Standard Locomotive Group set about evaluating the engines of the old Big Four in order to decide which, if any, of their characteristics would be of use in the planned new designs. They arranged locomotive exchanges between the regions of British Railways and a very comprehensive amount of data was collected. The Stanier locomotives tested were said to have impressed the team leader, RA Riddles, the most.

It therefore came as no surprise to discover that his first major Standard Class locomotive owed more of its design detail to the best practices of the LMS than to those of any of the three other companies. The first new locomotive, numbered 70000 and named *Britannia,* was unveiled at Crewe in January 1951.

By October of that year there were 25 of the class in service when, unfortunately, all had to be withdrawn because driving wheels were observed to be shifting on the axles of some locomotives. The teething problems were very quickly rectified and the engines were soon to be seen operating on all BR regions, but they did not necessarily receive universal acclaim.

In fact, even within regions, performances and opinions varied greatly. For example, the Western Region had a complement of 15 Britannias and they were mainly shared between three depots, Cardiff Canton, Plymouth Laira and Old Oak Common. Cardiff was to report good results with the engines, but those findings were not echoed by the depot managers and enginemen at the two other steam sheds.

The Eastern Region initially received 14 of the class and they were shared between Stratford and Norwich depots, where they were given an enthusiastic welcome by the crews. Three of the class went to the Southern Region and, for a time, two locomotives, Nos 70004 *William Shakespeare* and 70014 *Iron Duke,* shared the prestigious 'Golden Arrow' boat train duties. The Midland Region had an

Britannia No 70004 *William Shakespeare* is reduced to shunting duties at a very down-at-heel Manchester Victoria station, 30 August 1967. Mike Stokes Archive

No 70000 *Britannia* returning to Crewe in the late evening having headed a return Crewe-Holyhead special. Author

Examples of the class preserved
No 70000 *Britannia*.
No 70013 *Oliver Cromwell*.
In August 2006 neither locomotive was in running order; both are the subject of ongoing restoration projects.

initial allocation of 12 engines and among their duties was the daily 'Irish Mail' service, for which five of the class were allocated to Holyhead.

The last batch of the class was allocated to Glasgow Polmadie depot to work Liverpool and Manchester trains. By the early months of 1964 the rapid spread of diesel was starting to force the Britannias away from the Western and Eastern Regions and, during the remainder of that year, all 55 of the class were allocated to the London Midland Region, with all but seven being sent to Carlisle Kingmoor depot.

A very grimy No 70015 *Apollo* is seen minus its nameplates but still with an original numberplate during the last throes of steam at Stockport Edgeley motive power depot in 1967. Mike Stokes Archive

No 70013 *Oliver Cromwell* seen on the West Coast Main Line at Moore in April 1968. Note that the authentic nameplates have been removed and painted names substituted. Author

ROYAL SCOT CLASS 4-6-0

A Scots guardsman stands guard over LMS 4-6-0 No 6115 *Scots Guardsman* at Liverpool Road station in 1980, during the Rocket 150 celebrations, two years after the engine's very brief two-charter heritage era main line career. Author

Power classification	7P
Built	Originally North British Locomotive Company, Glasgow and Derby Works between 1927 and 1930. 71 locomotives built and all named. LMS number sequence 6100-6170 (46100-46170).
Designer	Henry Fowler.
Rebuilt	1943-1955 during the rule of Sir WA Stanier for the London Midland & Scottish Railway, and thereafter by British Railways.

Examples of the class preserved
No 6100 *Royal Scot*.
No 6115 *Scots Guardsman*.
Both are reportedly earmarked for a return to steam

Although not strictly speaking a Crewe locomotive, the Royal Scot class in both original and rebuilt form were frequent visitors to the works and were often to be seen on West Coast Main Line express services. Listings for locomotives of the class allocated to Crewe North (5A) running shed showed six in 1950 and 17 in 1959, and among later jobs allocated to them were the London-Holyhead services.

The class came into being at a time when the LMS was extremely short of powerful express engines to take charge of its Anglo-Scottish expresses. The LMSR management had even arranged for a Great Western Castle Class 4-6-0 to undergo trials on the WCML in order to evaluate its performance, and the locomotive reportedly outperformed anything the LMSR had at the time.

What then followed, viewed with hindsight, looked like a severe case of GWR diplomatic flu! The LMSR

Leeds City station in August 1958 and 4-6-0 No 46103 *Royal Scots Fusilier* waits to back on to the 10.15 service to Glasgow. Jubilee 4-6-0 No 45568 *Western Australia* is seen taking water in the other platform.
Mike Stokes Archive

attempted to place an order for 50 Castle types with the Swindon workshops of the GWR, but the order was not accepted. This was supposedly because of the need to regauge the design to accommodate the then-existing LMSR limitations, which meant that the GWR would not, owing to its own workload, be able supply the engines! At that time a certain WA Stanier was an employee of the GWR; he did not join the LMSR until 1932.

The first of the powerful parallel-boilered Royal Scot locomotives was outshopped by the NBL Co in July 1927 and a total of 50 were put into service before the end of that year. Indeed, the class leader, No 6100 *Royal Scot*, hauled the first 'Royal Scot' train on 26 September 1927. The huge success in service of the first batch of engines meant that the company placed an order for a further 20, but this time with its own works at Derby.

It is widely thought that No 6100 *Royal Scot* went on an 11,194-mile tour of North America in 1933. In reality sister engine No 6152 *The Kings Dragoon Guardsman* undertook that trip, in the guise of No 6100. That locomotive spent some time in the works at Crewe in preparation for the stateside trip. Reportedly the locomotives resumed their own identities afterwards.

Stanier took the chassis of experimental locomotive No 6170 *Fury* — an apt name given that an exploding fire tube on the high pressure locomotive killed one footplateman and severely injured another in February 1930 — and used it in 1934 with his newly developed Type 2 taper boiler to create the locomotive No 6170 *British Legion*. That was the forerunner for the rebuilt Royal Scots, all with taper boilers, double blast pipes, new smoke boxes and new bogies.

Class 6 Clan 4-6-2

mixed traffic locomotives

Built at Crewe 1951-52 as a scaled-down version of the Britannia Class, these engines were intended for use on routes with axle loading restrictions that prohibited the use of Class 7 locomotives. The London Midland Region retained responsibility for the 10 engines in the class, but for operational purposes they were all allocated to the Scottish Region.

There were plans to build another 15 of the small Pacifics in 1952 and allocate five to the Southern Region and a further 10 to the Scottish Region, but the order was cancelled.

No member of the class has been preserved. However, there is a group based at the Swanage Railway who have declared their intention to build from scratch a standard gauge 4-6-2 Standard class 6 loco to be numbered 72010 and named *Hengist*.

No 72004 *Clan Macdonald* north of Harthope on Beattock Bank with a Carlisle-Glasgow stopping train, April 1959.

No 72005 *Clan Macgregor* pictured at Corkerhill Shed Glasgow, April 1955.
Both David Anderson

STANDARD CLASS 8 DUKE 4-6-2

Power classification	8P
Built	Crewe 1954, one locomotive, British Railways No 71000 named *Duke of Gloucester*.
Designer	BR Standard locomotive by a team led by RA Riddles at BR Derby.

No 71000 is pictured in the loop at Appleby during a 'Dalesman' run over the Settle & Carlisle railway.
David Gibson

That the 8P 4-6-2 standard Pacific was ever built at all is, in a way, down to an accident, in fact a serious and fatal railway accident.

During his time as CME of the LMS Stanier had, as an experimental move, built one of the company's Princess Royal class locomotives as a steam turbine-driven engine. No 6202 was fitted with turbines manufactured by Metropolitan Vickers and emerged from Crewe Works in 1935 to be known as the Turbomotive.

The locomotive ran in normal traffic in that guise until 1950, and it enjoyed a modicum of success before a decision was taken to convert it to a conventional Princess Royal and, as such, it was named *Princess Anne*. Shortly after re-entering service, the engine was involved in the horrific Harrow & Wealdstone crash in October 1952, and it was so badly damaged that a decision was taken to write it off. That act left a gap in the number of 8P Pacifics available to the London Midland Region of BR and Mr Riddles took that as the perfect opportunity to introduce his team's new standard 8P design.

Riddles gained special financing for the project, which was at first envisaged as being a modified Duchess 4-6-2 with four cylinders, a double blast pipe and chimney and built using bar frames. The locomotive, as built, was in reality a different concept altogether and emerged from the works as a three-cylinder engine, which was also a departure from BR Standard practice that hitherto had employed only two-cylinder designs on the smaller class 6 and 7 Pacific engines.

Perhaps the most striking difference to the lineside observer was the addition of British Caprotti rotary cam poppet valve gear to the cylinders, driven by shafts attached to the centre driving wheels and easily discernable to even the untutored eye. There has been a great deal written about the below-expectation early performances of this unique locomotive, and many of those problems reportedly centred on unsatisfactory draughting arrangements. The imminent end of steam on BR meant that no great effort was made to rectify the problems.

When withdrawn in 1962, after only eight years in BR service, *Duke of Gloucester* was earmarked to become a part of the National Collection, but that decision was reversed in favour of a move to keep only the cylinder assembly and valve gear. With those

Running repairs. *Duke of Gloucester* engineer Gary Shannon is pictured examining the inside cylinders of the locomotive. Author

Perhaps the most striking difference to the lineside observer was the addition of British Caprotti rotary cam poppet valve gear to the cylinders, driven by shafts attached to the centre driving wheels and easily discernable to even the untutored eye. It is clearly seen in this comparison picture with No 5690 *Leander*. Author

Early days in preservation the Duke is seen at the Great Central Railway in 1987. Author

parts removed, No 71000 was despatched to the Woodham Brothers' Barry scrapyard but escaped the cutting torches when bought and moved out of the yard in 1974 by the then-newly formed Duke of Gloucester Locomotive Trust.

The trust restored the engine to its former glory and it was declared finished in 1986 but, not content with that achievement, the trust then continued to perform further engineering miracles and the historically significant locomotive returned triumphantly to the main line in April 1990.

Following a second refurbishment at its East Lancashire Railway home base, the Duke is in 2006 enjoying a further successful period of main line and preserved railway running, and No 71000 is in a condition of which even the original design team and builders would be justifiably proud.

What is for sure is that the engine as rebuilt by its enthusiastic and skilled owning group is now fulfilling all the expectations of its design team, and more! Having had the time, expertise and money to modify No 71000, the owning trust is sure that it now rightly deserves to be described as the 'world's most advanced steam locomotive'.

Standard Class 8P

A single locomotive in the class was built at Crewe in 1954 and given the British Railways number 71000 and the name *Duke of Gloucester*. It was then, and is still, a unique steam locomotive. The exceptional engine has in preservation proved conclusively that the design team led by RA Riddles at BR Derby and the build team at Crewe almost certainly created the world's most advanced steam locomotive.

No 71000 is pictured back in Crewe works on Saturday 24 July 2004 having been repainted to a very high standard, under contract by Bombardier.

The locomotive is seen as finished, before painting and also in primer while in the paint booth at Crewe Works.

All pictures Author.

4-6-2

Crewe-built steam locomotive types

LMS Jubilee Class 4-6-0

Power classification	5XP (later BR 6P5F)
Built	Between 1934 and 1936 at Derby (10), North British Locomotive Works, Glasgow (50) and Crewe (131) – 191 built in total. LMS number sequence 5552-5742 (BR 45552-45742)
Designer	William Stanier for the London Midland & Scottish Railway.

Passing Penmaenmawr on the Welsh Coast, preserved Crewe-built Jubilee 4-6-0 No 5690 *Leander* makes a fine sight. Brian Jones

Preserved example No 5596 *Bahamas* 'in the red' at the now-defunct Dinting Rail Centre, November 1969. Author

Three members of this large class of locomotives had the distinction of representing the last of Stanier's express passenger steam locomotives to run regularly in the UK. Withdrawn in 1967, they were thus in service for more than 30 years, a great accolade for a design that was initially said to be less-than-perfect.

The need of the LMS for this type of engine was so serious that the first batch was ordered straight off the drawing board without any prototype being built or running trials taking place. The designer's intention was to combine the best features of the Patriot class three-cylinder locos with the developments that had been incorporated in the then-recently introduced two-cylinder 'Black Five'.

Owing to problems associated with superheating, emphasised by the Jubilee's supposedly poor draughting characteristics that were, at the time, described as ill-proportioned, the new class was initially received less than favourably by some engine crews. A great amount of investigation did take place, and the problems were identified.

However, it was not until No 5665 *Lord Rutherford of Nelson* emerged from Crewe Works, with 113 of the 5XPs already in service, that the engineers were acknowledged finally to have solved the problems.

The most noteworthy performances of these widely allocated engines were those undertaken on services connecting Leeds with both Bristol and Glasgow. They were also noted as having been impressive performers on Midland main line express services between London St Pancras and Manchester, and also north of the border on trains to Girvan and Stranraer via the famous 'Port Road'.

In 1948 the whole class was taken into BR ownership. The first to be scrapped was No 45637 *Windward Islands,* which was involved in the tragic Harrow and Wealdstone crash in 1952 and damaged beyond repair.

BR began withdrawing the locomotives in 1960 and, happily, four have survived into preservation.

Preserved example No 5593 *Kolhapur* seen in September 1988 at the Severn Valley Railway. Author

Back in the works and proud to be there! No 5690 *Leander* arrives in good time for The Great Gathering. Author

Seen at Willesden (1A) is rebuilt Jubilee No 45735 *Comet*, pictured in 1960.
Mike Stokes Archive

No 45563 *Australia* is seen heading 'down the coast' away from Chester in September 1965. Note the nameplate is missing and the yellow cabside stripe denoting that the engine could not work south of Crewe 'under the wires'. Author

Examples of the class preserved
No 45593 (5593) *Kolhapur,* built by the North British Locomotive Works in the company of her sister loco
No 45596 (5596) *Bahamas*
No 45699 (5699) *Galatea* is a Crewe-built example, as is
No 45690 (5690) *Leander,* which entered traffic in 1936.

Crewe-built No 45647 *Sturdee* double-heads out of Leeds City in August 1966 with NBL-built No 45562 *Alberta*.

Another Crewe-built locomotive, No 45674 *Duncan* arrives in Sheffield in 1963.

Birmingham New Street in 1961 and Crewe product No 45556 *Nova Scotia* passes through a centre road with a non-stopping train.
All Mike Stokes Archive

Made in Crewe

Looking Back

The railway at Crewe in years past

The approach to Crewe station seen from the North Junction signal cabin in April 1881.

Crewe South Junction viewed on 10 January 1916.

A MINISTERIAL VISIT TO
the Works

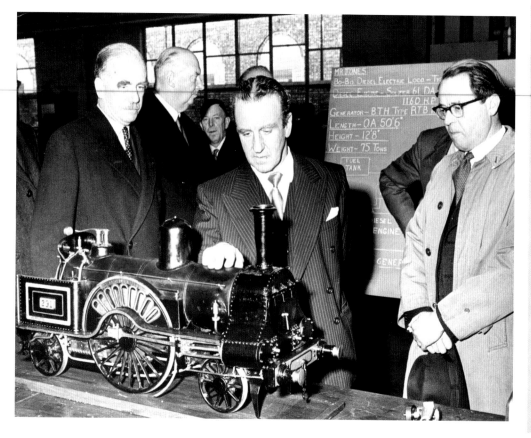

A 1960s visit to the works and the Apprentice School by Ernest Marples, the Conservative Minister of Transport. He is 'patting the engine' in the top picture.

He brought in STD (Subscriber Trunk Dialling), roadside yellow lines, parking meters and seat belts.

It was also under Ernest Marples that Dr Beeching was appointed to cut the British railway system down by two-thirds. And, oh yes, there was something else!

Ernest Marples (later to become Baron Marples of Wallasey) was also a road builder. His once-prominent company was Marples, Ridgeway & Partners. When it was pointed out to him that the road-building connection did not sit well with his position as Minister of Transport he sold his shares in the firm — to his wife!

On retirement he went to live in Malta where he died in 1978.

Both pictures Crewe Works Archive.

Monks Coppenhall Junction
before Crewe Works existed

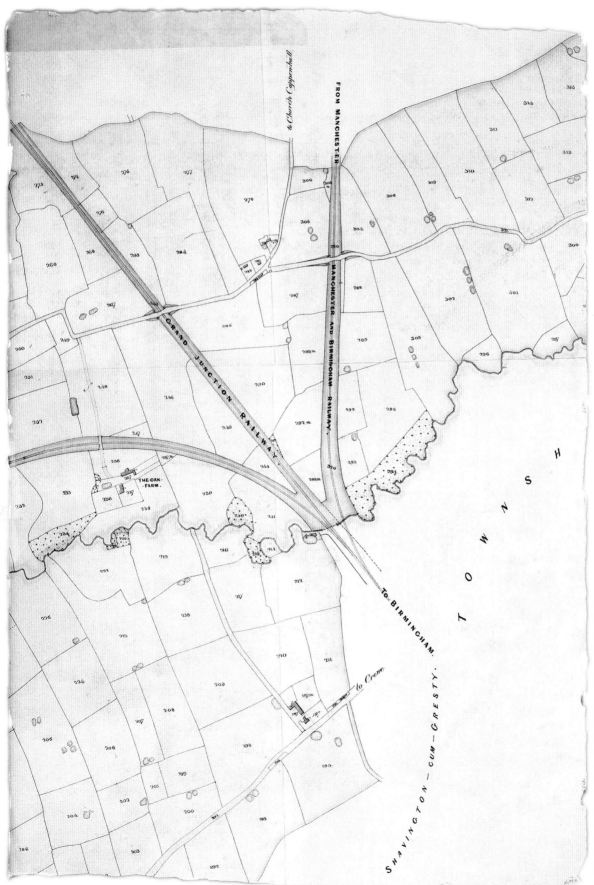

Section of a very old map lent by Cheshire Archives shows clearly the 'Grand Junction' without the works or any private house in sight. The map was drawn in1839 and shows the line to Chester curving away to the left past a collection of buildings called The Oak Farm while the Grand Junction Railway is shown as going north and passing under the road noted as leading to Church Coppenhall. The Manchester and Birmingham is drawn curving away to the right.

LMS CLASS 5MT 'BLACK FIVE' 4-6-0

Power classification	5P5F (later BR 5MT)
Built	Between 1934 and 1951 by Armstrong Whitworth & Co (327), Vulcan Foundry (100), Derby (100), Horwich (105) and Crewe Works (210) – 842 built in total. LMS number series 4658-5499 (BR 44658-45499).
Designer	William A Stanier for the London Midland & Scottish Railway.

Preserved locomotive No 4767 (44767) *George Stephenson* at home on the North Yorkshire Moors Railway. It was built at Crewe and fitted with Stephenson link motion.
Author

Almost every popular adjective has been applied to descriptions of this type of mixed traffic locomotive with the most appropriate possibly being 'ubiquitous'.

Being so numerous a class, they really did appear to be everywhere at once and justifiably were considered to be the LMS 'maids of all work'. During their long working lives they were just as likely to be found on a main line express as busy shunting wagons for a pick-up goods on a branch line.

The real success story of the design undoubtedly stemmed from its route availability as the 'Black Five's weight and length gave it the freedom to range over almost all of the LMS system and elsewhere.

As with the Jubilees, this new-build design was urgently needed by the LMS and, accordingly, the first batch was also ordered straight off the drawing board without a prototype engine being trialled. But, unlike the Jubilees, these two-cylinder locomotives were a success right from the start. Modifications to the type were, of course, made as production began, but the basic design had proved to be sound and the locos were almost universally popular with footplate crews.

The first of the class to enter service was, in fact, the 21st in the number sequence, No 5020, which left the works of Vulcan Foundry, Newton-le-Willows, in August 1934. This, in fact, reportedly caused more than a little embarrassment at Crewe Works, which did not turn out their first 'Five', the designated class leader No 5000, until the spring of the following year. The record for the largest single order placed by a railway company concerned 227 engines of this class and was awarded to Tyneside engineers Armstrong Whitworth.

Preserved 'Black Five' No 45305 attracts a lot of attention as it arrives in Crewe Works during The Great Gathering, September 2005. Brian Wilson

'Black Fives' preserved; final BR numbers,
year of build and builder shown in brackets:
Nos 44767 (Crewe 1947), 44806 (Derby 1944), 44871, 44901 (Crewe 1945),
44932 (Horwich 1945), 45000 (Crewe 1935), 45025 (Vulcan Foundry 1934),
45110 (Vulcan Foundry 1935), 45163, 45212 (Armstrong Whitworth 1935),
45231, 45293 (Armstrong Whitworth 1936), 45305, 45337, 45379, 45407,
45428 (Armstrong Whitworth 1937), 45491 (Derby 1943).

HG Ivatt, during his time as CME of the LMS, saw fit to produce no less than 11 experimental versions of the 'Black Five'. Withdrawal of the class started in 1961 and No 45401 was the first but, significantly, seven years later, on 4 August 1968, it was 'Black Five' No 45212 that had the dubious honour of hauling the last timetabled steam train for British Railways. The following week is well remembered by enthusiasts as three 'Black Fives', Nos 44781, 44871 and 45110, were involved in the last rites that officially commemorated the end of the steam era on BR (together with Britannia Class No 70013 *Oliver Cromwell*).

Stanier was correct and to the point when he described the 'Black Five' as being 'a deuce of a good engine' so he would no doubt have been pleased to know that no less than 18 of the locomotives have made it into preservation, the vast majority of which have been steamed again.

Another preserved Crewe-built 'Black Five' No 5000 (45000) hard at work on the Severn Valley Railway, April 1984. Author

An Armstrong Whitworth built engine No 45426 at Preston Brook, near Warrington, in April 1960. This engine was withdrawn in March 1968.
Author's collection

Crewe-built No 44973 in the Scottish Highlands, heading south at Tyndrum in 1959. This locomotive was withdrawn in September 1965.

Crewe-built No 44727, an example with a steel firebox, arriving at Manchester Victoria in August 1967. This locomotive was withdrawn in October 1967.

Crewe-built No 45457 seen at Perth in 1963. This locomotive was withdrawn in September 1963. All Mike Stokes Archive

STANIER CLASS 5 2-6-0 (MOGUL)

Power classification	5MT (Mixed Traffic) later BR 6P5F
Built	Between 1933 and 1934 at Crewe Works – 40 built in total. Numbered 2945-2984 (BR 42945-42984)
Designer	William A Stanier for the London Midland & Scottish Railway.

Following on from the highly successful 'Crab' moguls, the LMS in 1933 ordered a further class of 2-6-0s to complement their stock of mixed traffic locomotives. The company's chief mechanical engineer, William Stanier, took inspiration for the design of this class from GWR moguls built at Swindon Works.

The first member of the class numbered as 13245 emerged from Crewe Works on 21 October 1933. The engine was married up to a six-wheel, Fowler-designed tender, as Stanier's own tender design had not at that time been completed. From that date until March 1939 the class continued to be outshopped from Crewe Works, 40 engines being built. Construction was postponed in order to make way for the imminent and intensive 'Black Five' building programme.

On first entering traffic, the Stanier moguls were sent in batches to each of the four LMS regions as they became available. The Northern-based examples worked into Scotland regularly over the ex-Caledonian line from their base at Carlisle Kingmoor depot. Eventually most of the class became concentrated on the Western Division of the company, and were allocated to the depots at Crewe South, Mold Junction and Nuneaton. Although the locomotives were principally thought of as freight engines, they did work very successfully on passenger services.

One locomotive from this popular type of Crewe-built moguls has survived into preservation. When new in 1934, it was numbered 13268 and was first allocated to Willesden depot. The mogul was later given the LMS number 2968 and then the BR number 42968. During the 1960s run-down of steam, the locomotive was sent to various depots including Gorton, Manchester and Heaton Mersey, Stockport.

At the end of its BR career it was to be found at Wigan Springs Branch shed and from there retired in December 1966. Sold for scrap in April 1967, it was fortunately rescued by the Stanier Mogul Fund in 1973 and moved to the Severn Valley Railway, where a full restoration was carried out. On 13 April 1991 the engine hauled a special train for members of the fund from Bridgnorth to Kidderminster to celebrate its return to traffic.

The mogul, in addition to being a regular performer at the SVR, has played a starring role in several memorable main line excursions.

November 1997 and No 2968 leads GWR mogul No 7325 up the famous Lickey Incline, a preservation first. Author

Heading for The Railway Age at Crewe prior to a main line working, No 2968 with its support coach passes through Crewe station. Author

No 42968 seen on the famous Crewe Works traverser. Author

LMS Ivatt Class 2, 2-6-0

Power classification	2P/2F, later 2MT
Built	Between 1946 and 1953 at Darlington (38), Swindon (25) and Crewe Works (65). 128 in total. BR numbered 46400-46527.
Designer	HG Ivatt for the LMS.

Crewe-built Ivatt 2-6-0 No 46441 glints in the evening sunlight after its arrival at 'The Works', 5 September 2005. Author

No 46521 illustrating the real branch line look at the Severn Valley Railway. Author

No 6441 displayed on the turntable at Carnforth, when new in preservation, June 1969. Author

In the years that immediately followed the Second World War, the LMS was quite well off with regard to its overall stock of locomotives following the Stanier building boom. It was, however, short of lightweight designs needed for use on weight-restricted secondary and branch lines. Those routes had hitherto relied on the older stock of small locomotives, many which were inherited at the time of Grouping and, by 1946, were well past their best.

To correct the situation Ivatt, in his position as chief mechanical engineer for the LMS, set about designing a locomotive within the class 2 power range to take over this essential work.

He decided to draw up plans for two classes of locomotive at the same time. Both would be class 2-rated but one would be a 2-6-0 tender locomotive and the other a 2-6-2 tank engine. To make future maintenance easier, the two types were fitted with many standard components, which included a Swindon-type taper boiler with a separate dome and top feed.

The locomotives were built with labour-saving in mind, and crews enjoyed the provision of rocking grates, self-emptying ash pans, self-cleaning smokeboxes and side-window cabs. To facilitate reverse running in the absence of turntables on many secondary lines, the tender cab and bunker were designed to give the crews good vision and also provide maximum comfort.

Initially the new 2-6-0s did not live up to their designer's expectations but, after experiments concerning draughting were concluded satisfactorily and modifications carried out, the moguls were able to show what fine, efficient and, indeed, speedy machines they were.

When nationalisation took place in 1948, only 20 of these locomotives had been built for the LMS but the newly formed British Railways continued with their construction for a further five years and, by the end of 1953, there were 128 in service. Crewe Works was responsible for building half the class and, in 1947, engine No 6417 (46417) had the distinction of becoming the last locomotive built at Crewe under LMS rule.

The engines were very successful and were not confined to LMS territory — five went to the Eastern Region, 13 to the North Eastern Region and 25 to the Western Region. The first of the class to be withdrawn was No 46407 in 1961, with 39 lasting until 1967. They have been described as the ideal locomotive for use on a preserved railway and, fortunately, seven have been saved.

Examples of the class preserved
All Crewe-built examples.
Nos 46428, 46441, 46443, 46447, 46464, 46512, 46521.

Patriot Class 6P/7P 4-6-0
'Baby Scots'

One of the greatest regrets among railway enthusiasts is the fact that not one single member of the 52-engine 'iconic' Patriot class was saved for preservation. 'Baby Scots' was a colloquial name for the 4-6-0 Patriot class locomotives designed by Sir Henry Fowler for the LMS, many of which included components from scrapped LNWR Claughton class engines. Between 1946 and 1949, 18 of the Patriot Class were rebuilt with LMS 2A boilers. The pet name was used because these locomotives in their original form looked like a smaller version of Fowler's famous Royal Scot class engines.

No 45541 *Duke of Sutherland* at Rugby in 1960.

No 45546 *Fleetwood* at Crewe South (5B) in 1961.

Rebuilt example No 45521 *Rhyl* on the turntable at Morecambe in 1963.
All pictures Author's Collection

Crewe-built steam locomotive types
LMS Class 8F, 2-8-0

Power classification	8F
Built	Between 1935 and 1946 by contractors Beyer-Peacock, North British Locomotive Co and Vulcan Foundry and at BR Works at Ashford, Brighton, Darlington, Doncaster, Eastleigh, Horwich, Swindon and Crewe – 852 built in total.
Designer	William Stanier for the London Midland & Scottish Railway.

No 48773 at home on the SVR. This is the engine that came back from war service. Author

Their ageing fleet of freight engines being at the time almost totally inadequate for the volume of work it faced in the 1930s led the LMS to seek a design of modern heavy goods locomotive that would solve all its problems. Stanier came up with his new 8F 2-8-0, which was hailed a winner right from the moment that the first example went into traffic in 1935.

Stanier had taken the experience gained in the construction of his highly successful 'Black Five' class and applied those criteria in a scaled-up form to his new freight locomotive. The 8Fs, in addition to fulfilling all that was required of them on freight duties, were found also to ride well at speed and some were consequently used on passenger trains running at speeds of up to 60mph. They had spacious cabs and their reliability ensured a regional acceptability by both engine crews and depot managers.

The advent of the Second World War saw the 8Fs pressed into intensive service not only at home but also overseas, and the Stanier 8F became Britain's 'engine of war'.

The wartime Government ordered that 208 of the engines be constructed by Beyer Peacock and the North British Locomotive Company, and requisitioned a further 51 from the LMS, shipping the whole batch overseas.

Several were lost at sea aboard torpedoed ships but the majority made it to the Middle East and, after being converted to oil burners, served on vital supply routes ranging as far afield as the Soviet Union.

At the time of railway nationalisation in 1948, all the British-based 8Fs were taken into stock by the London Midland Region and 39 engines returned from overseas duty. Many, however, stayed abroad and worked in Egypt, Iran, Iraq, Israel, Italy, Turkey and the Lebanon, with some locomotives working

The author's home town of Northwich was a good place to see 8Fs as they were regularly used on the limestone trains between the ICI works at Winnington, Lostock and the quarry at Buxton. That service, although in a reduced form, is still running in 2006 powered, of course, by modern traction. Author's Collection

Three years before the end of steam, 8F 2-8-0 No 48544 looks to be in good external order at Buxton MPD, December 1965. Author's Collection

The West Coast Railways 8F arrives at Crewe via the works main line connection and access line. Author

well into the 1980s. In 1957 British Railways held a stock of 666 and, in the main, they continued to serve the company well right to the end of the steam era.

Locomotive No 48616 became the first to be scrapped following a derailment in 1960 and withdrawals proper began with No 48009 leading the way to the scrapyards in 1962. Approximately 150 examples survived into the last year of BR steam and the last two retired were Nos 48318 and 48773 from Rose Grove depot in Lancashire, on 4 August 1968.

Examples of the class preserved
Nos 48151(8151)*, 48173 (8173)*, 48305(8305)*, 48431(8431), 48513, 48624, 48773†
*Crewe-built locomotives. †Repatriated from Turkey.

No 48151 is moved on the Crewe Works 'Traverser'. The pouring rain adds to the atmosphere of the shot. Author

Preserved Crewe-built Stanier 8F No 48151 is currently owned and operated by the West Coast Railway Co Ltd who are to be congratulated on the excellent condition in which it was sent 'back home' to The Great Gathering. The engine is seen on the ash pit in the works, buffered up to LNER B1 4-6-0 No 61264. Author

BR STANDARD CLASS 9F, 2-10-0

Power classification	9F
Built	Between 1954 and 1960 at Swindon (53) and Crewe Works (198) – 251 built in total. BR number series 92000-92250.
Designer	BR Standard locomotive by a team at Derby led by RA Riddles, for British Railways.

1958 Crewe-built locomotive No 92049 heads for Shotton Steel Works from Chester in September 1965. Author

In Crosti form, Crewe-built No 92028 is seen in 1958 the year conversions back to normal draughting commenced. The engine's chimney was used only on 'light up' and the exhaust exited via a multiple blast pipe and long thin chimney (under the odd-looking smoke deflector) on the side of the locomotive. Author's Collection

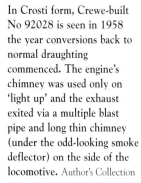

Did the BR Standard design team keep their best for last or had they simply become even more expert with experience? Whatever the reason the 9F, the 12th of their designs, is, with hindsight, regarded as the most successful of the Standard class locos. A locomotive of the class holds the distinction of being the last steam locomotive built by British Railways and, accordingly, No 92220 was painted in lined green livery and named Evening Star when outshopped from Swindon Works in March 1960.

Circumstances dictated that this impressive class would have only a short service life, but even that small number of years was sufficient time to prove the worth of the mighty 2-10-0s. In fact, the examples saved have now been in preserved ownership longer than they were in BR ownership.

The design team had been faced with the problems of making a very large '10 coupled' engine available for use on the maximum number of routes – a difficult task. The 21ft 8in wheelbase had to be capable of following tight curves and, to achieve this, the team designed the centre pair of driving wheels without flanges and additionally the axle loading was kept low at only 15 tons 10cwt.

The locomotives were designed for use on the heaviest of freight trains at reasonably high speeds and, when in service, they often also worked passenger trains at speeds reported to be between 80 and 90mph, an incredible achievement for an engine with only 5ft diameter driving wheels. Real pulling power was the main asset of the Standard Class 9s. With great success the 9Fs worked heavy iron ore trains from the docks at Newport in south Wales to the region's blast furnaces. Similar workings took place from Birkenhead Docks on Merseyside to Shotton steelworks in north Wales.

The Tyne Dock-to-Consett workings were perhaps the hardest regular tasks undertaken by the class, and those iron ore trains could weigh up to 787 tons each. In addition they had to be hauled up gradients as steep as 1 in 35, a task that proved well within the capabilities of the sure-footed Standard 9Fs working in pairs. It was, after all, the kind of work Riddles had in mind when he envisaged the design.

'If it isn't broke, don't fix it' is a statement that could, with hindsight, have been attributed to the Crosti boiler experiment carried out on Nos 92020-29 in 1955. The design team wanted to experiment with the Italian system in an attempt firstly to save on coal and secondly make lower-quality coal usable.

More than one commentator has since used the word disastrous when talking about the outcome of

Preserved National Collection engine No 92220 *Evening Star* passes Delamere on the Cheshire Lines heading for Chester, in July 1985. Author

No 92008, one of the first batch built at Crewe, is seen leaving Northwich for Chester in May 1961.
Mike Stokes Archive

the experiments. The Crosti system was later abandoned (beginning in 1958) and the 10 engines continued in service thereafter with a smaller boilers and fireboxes, and therefore had smaller evaporative capacity. They were allocated duties that did not call for high boiler output, but externally they in part retained the 'Crosti look'.

Crewe-built locomotives numbering 92165-92167 were fitted with mechanical stokers to an American design in 1958, and this modification showed some advantages in being able to increase the firing rate above that achievable by a fireman with a shovel. Increased evaporation could be achieved and thus heavier trains could, if required, be hauled at higher speeds. The equipment was, in any event, removed from the three engines in 1962 and one of them, No 92167, survived as the last 9F in service, in 1968.

Examples of the class preserved
Nos 92134*, 92203 *Black Prince*†, 92207, 92212, 92214, 92219, 92220 *Evening Star*, 92240*, 92245*
*Crewe-built locos †Name given in preservation.
No 92134, which is in the process of being restored, is expected to steam again in 2007, which will mark 50 years since it left Crewe Works.

A Crosti-boilered loco No 92022 (Crewe-built) that has been converted back to normal draughting is seen at Stockport in 1967.
Mike Stokes Archive

Under restoration Standard Class 9F 2-10-0 No 92134 is positioned for display in the Crewe erecting shops prior to the Great Gathering. Author

HUGHES/FOWLER 'CRAB' 2-6-0

Power classification	5F (BR 6P5F)
Built	Between 1926 and 1932 at Horwich (70) and Crewe (175) First numbered 13000-13244, renumbered as 42700-42944 in 1934-36.
Designer	Hughes/Fowler

'Crab' 2-6-0 No 42863
at Walsden in 1961,
the day the station closed.
Authors Collection

Crewe works turned out its first batch of 2-6-0 'Crabs' in 1925-26 and those LMS Moguls followed on from the first batch, which were built at Horwich Works. Crewe-built locomotive numbered 13178 (renumbered as 42878) was officially declared as being the 6000th engine built as Crewe. In reality that accolade should, according to some records, perhaps have been awarded to a Fowler 7F 0-8-0 No 9517 (49517) built in 1929.

The mogul type of wheel arrangement originated in the USA during the mid-1850s and the configuration

June 1964 pictures of
Mogul Nos 42942 and
42710 respectively, at
Stockport (Edgeley) MPD.
Both Mike Stokes Archive

was not commonly exploited in the early years of UK locomotive building. The chief mechanical engineer of the LMSR from 1923 to 1925 (he was formerly CME of the Lancashire & Yorkshire Railway and subsequently LNWR) George Hughes designed what observers have since described as an excellent mixed traffic locomotive of the Mogul type. Much of the design work was carried out by Hughes's old team at Horwich Works and in many respects the resultant loco incorporated a great many L&Y features.

The design was certainly 'different' as with their two outside cylinders set at an inclined angle the front running board of the engines needed to be raised accordingly. Hughes called for an 180psi parallel boiler to be used and that appeared to 'squat' between the frames and in conjunction with the raised running board resulted in the engines being given the name 'Crabs', a title that stuck!

When construction of these engines got under way in 1926 Mr Hughes had retired and so supervision of the build was undertaken by his successor Henry Fowler (later Sir Henry). The basic design was left unchanged but Fowler did introduce some 'Midland Railway' style changes. The most noticeable being the replacement of the originally intended L&Y tender with a 3500-gallon Midland tender, even though those units were quite a bit narrower than the engine proper.

In 1931 five engine of the type were experimentally rebuilt with Lentz rotary cam poppet valves and that gear was in turn replaced by Reidinger rotary poppet valve gear during 1953. (42818/22/24/25/29). In 1961 members of the class started to be withdrawn from service but several stayed in use almost until the end of the steam era.

Examples of the class preserved
13000 in the guise of LMSR No 2700
42765 based at the East Lancashire Railway
         and has run in preservation
42859 which is currently in unrestored condition.

On the belt!

Three stages in the construction of a Hughes/Fowler 2-6-0 5MT 'Crab' in Crewe Works. This is thought to be No 13178 (42878) the official 6000th Crewe built locomotive (June 1930). The 'Belt' was Crewe's version of a production line. Crewe Works Archive

Visitors to *the Works*

LITTLE AND LARGE!

A visitor of an entirely different kind: this huge locomotive is one of 33 Beyer-Garratt-type locomotives that were operated by the LMS and were built 1927-1930 by Beyer Peacock. No 47998 is one of the earlier locomotives and is seen in original condition fitted with a straight-sided coal bunker (as was sister locomotive No 47999) All the others (Nos 47967-47997) were built with revolving coal bunkers. The 2-6-6-2T locomotives were all allocated to Crewe Works for service and repair. Author's Collection

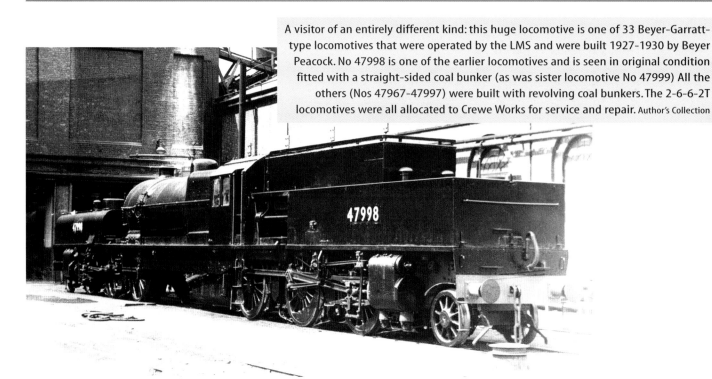

A selection of
Crewe-built tank locomotives

LNWR 0-6-2 tank loco
No 252 dating from about 1881.

BR 2-6-2 tank loco No 41310
seen at Bath in 1964.
There were 130 of these
engines built (Derby 10 and
Crewe 120). No 41272 was
the official 7000th Crewe-built
engine and in service carried
commemorative plaques.

BR 2-6-2 tank locomotive
No 84001 seen at Llandudno
Junction in 1963. Crewe built
20 of these engines including
the one shown and Darlington
Works built a further 10.
All Author's Collection

Webb Crewe Works Charity Fund
– The Great Gathering

North British-built AC electric No 84001 (E3035) from the NRM waits to be positioned for display. Author

A Fragonset-liveried Class 31 arrives at the 'works' with FM Rails' No 47832 in tow. Author

The September 2005 Great Gathering event at the Bombardier Crewe Works site was a triumph of organisation and thankfully a real financial success story. The obvious question on everyone's lips afterwards was would the 'works' ever play host to another Great Gathering?

There are several future railway preservation milestones with Crewe connections that could collectively or separately form the basis of special enthusiast events. There are other sites for special railway heritage events and they of course include the National Railway Museum at York. However the lure of another visit to the world-famous Crewe Locomotive Works would once again be seen as an exceptionally attractive prospect, by both family groups and railway enthusiasts.

Both preserved Britannia class locomotives No 70000 *Britannia* and No 70013 *Oliver Cromwell* are set to return to steam. Those connected with the project to re-streamline Crewe-built Stanier Pacific No. 46229 *Duchess of Hamilton* (for static exhibit purposes) have stated that they aim to have the locomotive back in the 1937 Coronation Scot design in time for the 70th anniversary of the class in 2007.

The month of August during the following year, 2008, marks the passing of 40 years since the official end of steam on BR. The same year marks 50 years since the last steam locomotive was built at Crewe Works. That engine was Standard 9F 2-10-0 No 92250, which was rolled out of the workshops in December 1958, unfortunately the locomotive is not among the preserved examples.

The management of Bombardier Transportation were quick to congratulate the organisers of the 2005 event and they acknowledged its high public relations value. It will be the future plans that Bombardier have outlining the role that Crewe Works will play in the international firm's overall scheme of things that will decide whether or not the works is able to play host to another such weekend.

When planning the 2005 event the Crewe site was ideal, having then many large and clean workshop areas, good footpaths and roadways and perhaps more importantly a main line connection. Also of great importance is the 'Traverser' without which the widespread positioning of the exhibited locomotives would be extremely difficult. In the months following the event Bombardier Transportation communications department, based at their Derby

United Kingdom HQ, had this to say on the subject of another event.

"At this time the overall future role of the Crewe site is under review following the company's' recent announcement of their intention not to sell the facility. It would be wrong at this stage to pre-empt the outcome of the review, and also try to second guess at any decisions that may be taken by the Crewe site's new management team. As there is reportedly a will on the part of the Webb Crewe Works Charity Fund to consider another event the Bombardier management team would in the future look at such a proposal in the light of the prevailing circumstances."

It can be easily appreciated that the company would be rightly reluctant to promise anything that they could not later deliver. If the new plans

Friday evening of 9 September 2005. And still they come! While the Llangollen Railways' 0-6-0ST *Jessie* prepares to move the giant by comparison No 71000 away from the coaling point, No 60009 A4 Pacific *Union of South Africa* arrives via the works' main line connection. Meanwhile, the 'logistical crew' discuss their next move, from left to right Glyn Henshall, Steve Blackburn and Lee Johnson. Author

What's the old saying? 'No show without Punch' The NRM's flagship steam locomotive No 4472 *Flying Scotsman* arrives for the Great Gathering with two diesel exhibits in tow, No 45112 *The Royal Army Ordnance Corps* and D1023 *Western Fusilier.* Author

Many of the locomotives exhibited at the GG were brought in by road. Heanor Heavy Haulage is pictured unloading the Co-Bo D5705 which it has brought from the East Lancashire Railway. Author

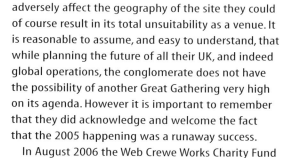

Class 40 number 40145 (D345) built by Vulcan Foundry in 1961 arrives at the 'works' by rail from the East Lancashire Railway. Author

Late into the night on Friday, and they kept arriving for the 'Gathering'. Ex-GWR 4-6-0 No 5972 *Olton Hall* (aka *Hogwarts Castle*) with No 46229 *Duchess of Hamilton* in tow waits to be 'coaled' while ex-Southern Railway Battle of Britain Pacific No 34067 *Tangmere* arrives ex main line direct from Stewarts Lane depot. Author

adversely affect the geography of the site they could of course result in its total unsuitability as a venue. It is reasonable to assume, and easy to understand, that while planning the future of all their UK, and indeed global operations, the conglomerate does not have the possibility of another Great Gathering very high on its agenda. However it is important to remember that they did acknowledge and welcome the fact that the 2005 happening was a runaway success.

In August 2006 the Web Crewe Works Charity Fund committee were still awaiting a final audit of their accounts, following the collection and correlation of all monies including gift aid. But they were able to announce that the final profit from the Great Gathering would approach an incredible £90,000. Several local charities and the preserved railways that supported the event would all benefit proportionately by the way of donations, after professional fees have been disbursed. Since the advent of railway privatisation in 1989 the charity has commendably raised over £250,000.

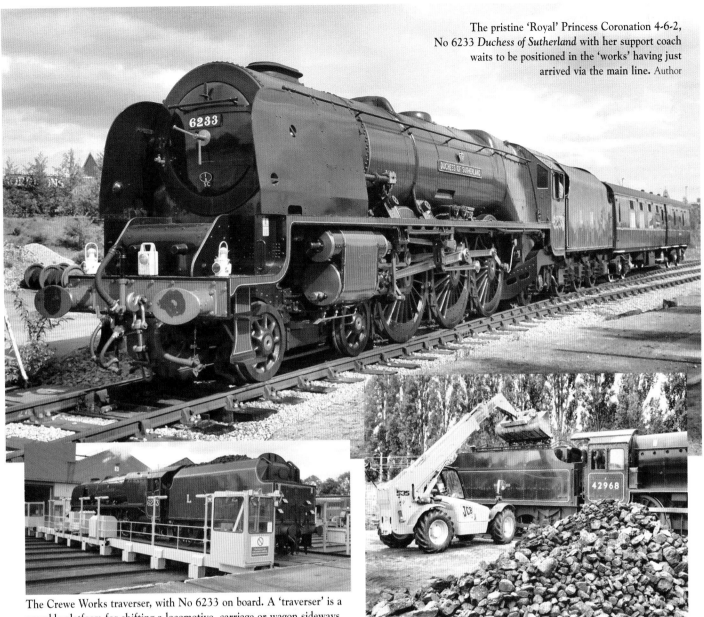

The pristine 'Royal' Princess Coronation 4-6-2, No 6233 *Duchess of Sutherland* with her support coach waits to be positioned in the 'works' having just arrived via the main line. Author

The Crewe Works traverser, with No 6233 on board. A 'traverser' is a movable platform for shifting a locomotive, carriage or wagon sideways from one running track to another. Used in railway workshops and formerly in passenger stations. The 'works' example is a particularly fine one and is in use constantly. Author

Steam locomotives need coal! And lots of it, Glyn Henshall loads up Severn Valley based Stanier 2-6-0 No 42968 from the temporary coaling facility created especially for the GG event. Author

All of that fundraising is only made possible by the selfless efforts of a great many volunteers, the majority working for many months and out of public view to ensure that the event would take place safely and be a success. In addition to those committee members and volunteers, three preserved railways, the Churnet Valley, East Lancashire and Llangollen and one narrow gauge railway, the Ffestiniog, provided hands-on help.

Such a huge event would have been impossible to organise without the practical support of the many locomotive owning groups and the UK railway industry in general. The movement of so many items of railway rolling stock to Crewe in time for the 'Gathering' was in its own right a logistical triumph and thanks must go to Steve Blackburn and his team who put in time and effort well beyond the normal call of duty. That team was well served by the management and professional locomotive crews of West Coast Railway Company Ltd, who faultlessly accomplished all the 'main line' rail movements to and from the 'works'.

Under the cover of darkness! The dual identity GWR visitor tows the 'not in steam' Crewe product No 46229 *Duchess of Hamilton* into the 'works'. Author

150 years of engineering excellence

Out of their time! Philip Hough (left) and
Mark O'Brien (right) pictured with the new boiler for
ex-LNER K4 No 61994. Both young men have served
a full apprenticeship with LNWR at Crewe. Author

Work starts on ex-BR Standard Class 7 4-6-2 Pacific
No 70000 *Britannia* at LNWR Heritage Co Ltd,
Crewe in July 2006. Nathan Patrick is seen relaying
hand signals to the crane driver during the boiler lift. Author

Steaming on!

Steam locomotive engineering is still alive and well in the town of Crewe. Popular music impresario and lifelong railway enthusiast Pete Waterman is the head of a company set up adjacent to the Railway Age at Crewe and fully equipped to repair locomotive boilers and fireboxes in general and steam locomotives in particular.

There are over 400 standard gauge steam locomotives preserved in the UK, and accordingly many of them are in regular service on our preserved railways. There is an obvious need for the specialist companies who have kept the old skills alive, and therefore are able to repair or completely rebuild those engineering wonders of a past age. Crewe based LNWR Heritage Company Limited is one of several such organisations.

The loss or dramatic shrinkage of heavy engineering manufacturing capabilities has reduced the opportunities for young people to learn the

techniques and skills associated with many processes and in particular those associated with steam engineering. The locomotive restoration companies and preserved railway workshops have, in albeit a limited way started to redress the balance.

Among manager Steve Latham's 20-strong team at LNWR Heritage are several young persons serving apprenticeships. The firm's time-served workforce now includes two young artisans who have completed their term of five year training with the company. It is encouraging that nationwide there are many youngsters working on preserved railway vehicles that were built and indeed taken out of service long before they were born!

In July 2006, Pete Waterman's company embarked upon a project to restore the iconic Crewe-built steam locomotive number 70000 *Britannia*. There is justice in the fact that Jeremy Hosking's 4-6-2 Pacific

Apprentice Ben Roberts is seen receiving instruction from steam engineer Bill Dakin. Author

No 70000 is now being rebuilt within a dedicated and specially equipped workshop adjacent to the site of the historic Crewe Loco Works, from which it emerged new in January 1951.

The new comprehensive rebuild of 70000 is expected to be a three-year project and it got under way in fine style when the LNWR Heritage-restored ex-British Railways Brighton depot 50-ton Cowans Sheldon works crane (ADRO 96719) joined forces with a hired-in 40-ton road crane in order to lift the boiler, and separate it from the rolling chassis. The locomotive boiler is a large 250lb per sq in standard type that carries the works number 805, and it is married to a wide firebox with a 42sq ft grate area.

When No 70000 is returned to main line operating condition, possibly in the summer of 2009, it is hoped that some of those great Britannia class performances of the late 50s and early 60s can be recreated. Notably the class were regularly seen hauling such named trains as 'The Hook Continental', 'The Bournemouth Belle', 'The Mancunian', 'The Irish Mail', 'The Ocean Liner Express' and of course the extremely prestigious 'Golden Arrow'.

The LNWR Heritage facility during 2006 was also busy repairing locomotives and boilers for various preserved railways and locomotive owners and that list included, Standard 9F 2-10-0 No 92134 (originally built Crewe 1957) ex-LNER K4 2-6-0 No 61994 The Great Marquess, ex-LMS Black Five No 45379, Ex-SR West Country 4-6-2 Pacific's No 34053 Sir Keith Park, No 34070 Manston and Merchant Navy No 35022 Holland-America Line. Ex-War Department 8F 2-8-0 No 90733 (Vulcan Foundry 5200) is nearing a return to steam and the following preserved ex-GWR locomotives are also going through the works, 4-6-0 No 7828 Odney Manor and tank engine Nos 1369, 4270 and 5541.

Ex-GWR 0-4-2T No 1450 was completely rebuilt at Pete Waterman's Crewe steam engineering works. It is pictured while being run in at the Churnet Valley Railway. Author

The company recently completed this new tender for ex-GWR No 6023 King Edward II. Author

Ex-SR 4-6-2 No 35022 Holland-America Line, which is now awaiting restoration at LNWR Heritage, is seen at work hauling Pullman Coaches on the Southern Region of BR in 1960. Mike Stokes Archive

CREWE
LOCOMOTIVE WORKS

MODERN TRACTION

by *Brian Sharpe*

The *Dawn* of *dieselisation*

Crewe Works may be synonymous with the age of steam, but British Railways abandoned steam in favour of more modern traction in the decade after 1955, and Crewe made a valuable contribution to BR's modernisation programme.

In fact, the LMS was at the forefront of the introduction of diesel locomotives with the 0-6-0 diesel shunters in service numbering no less than 71 by nationalisation in 1948.

Just before nationalisation, it was the LMS under HA Ivatt that introduced Britain's first main line diesel-electric locomotive, Co-Co No 10000, joined by its partner No 10001 in 1948, and a couple of other experimental designs. But, although Nos 10000 and 10001 were built by the LMS, it was at Derby, not Crewe.

Generally, Britain's traditional railway-owned workshops remained fairly conservative in outlook and carried on building and maintaining steam

locomotives. Britain's private locomotive builders, with their eyes more on the export trade, were more adventurous and had started building diesel locomotives much earlier, as parts of continental Europe and the USA, in particular, were years ahead of Britain in introducing diesels. It was these private builders who largely pioneered the construction of diesel locomotives for the domestic main line market, with diesel shunters coming from a variety of manufacturers at first, until production started at Derby Works.

But Nos 10000 and 10001, with 1600hp engines, were no match for Crewe's finest Pacifics and Crewe, like other BR workshops, stayed loyal to steam. The first real threat came from English Electric's prototype Deltic, a 3300hp Co-Co machine designed with the American market in mind, but which was tested on the West Coast Main Line through Crewe from 1955 onwards, and proved easily the equal of any steam engine — but at enormous cost.

Crewe's first diesel, D3419, was one of 135 0-6-0 shunters built at the works, and remained in service until July 1983 at Cardiff as No 08349, being scrapped at Swindon Works in 1986.
The Crewe Archive

Diesel-electric locomotive No 10001 was built by the LMS, but at Derby not Crewe.
Mike Stokes Archive

0-6-0 shunter No 09026
pictured at Brighton in 2000.
Mike Stokes Archive

In 1955 British Railways announced its modernisation plan. Even though there were just six reliable main line diesels in service, plus a selection of shunters, the future was to be diesel and electric — and quickly.

Even so, Crewe carried on building steam engines, but did finally dip its toe in the water of diesel production in 1957, when it turned out a 350hp 0-6-0 diesel-electric shunter, D3419. The later LMS-designed diesel shunters, developed in conjunction with English Electric, had been adopted by BR as standard for shunting engines, and no less than 1192 were built between 1952 and 1962, by different railway workshops, with engines and traction motors supplied by various contractors. Under BR's computerised TOPS system, they were designated Class 08, and many remain in service today, plus large numbers in preservation.

Crewe's D3419 was one of 135 eventually built at the works, and remained in service until July 1983 at Cardiff as No 08349, being scrapped at Swindon Works in 1986. It was one of a batch with an English Electric six-cylinder 350hp engine and two nose-suspended English Electric traction motors. The maximum tractive effort of 35,000lb compares with 40,000lb for a Duchess Pacific.

No 08873 shunting
Crewe station in
August 1996 was built
at BR Darlington. Author

Made in Crewe

D5030 new out of Crewe Works in 1959. Production of the class had commenced at Derby with D5000 in 1958 but locomotives D5030-65 and D5076-93 were Crewe-built in 1959-60. The Crewe Archive

Crewe's *first* main line *diesel*

t was soon time to build something bigger, though, and Crewe's very first main line diesel product was one of the classes of smaller pioneer main line diesels, a 1250hp diesel-electric Bo-Bo fitted with a Sulzer engine. Production of the class had commenced at Derby with D5000 in 1958, but D5030-65 and D5076-93 were Crewe-built in 1959-60.

Even these 54 engines were not exactly at the forefront of modern traction technology, being modestly powered machines designed for fairly mundane duties, but it clearly pointed to the way forward for Crewe Works. The future would be diesel and electric and, by the time D5093 emerged from the works in July 1960, Crewe had built its last steam engine.

Crewe's BR/Sulzer Type 2s went to work in East Anglia at first, mostly allocated to March shed. The engines that became Class 24 under the TOPS system nearly all ended their days working in the Crewe area in the late 1970s, their last front-line passenger duties being summer Saturday holiday extras to the Cambrian Coast. Of the Crewe-built members of the class, three are still in existence: D5032 and D5061 working on the North Yorkshire Moors Railway, and D5054 on the East Lancashire Railway.

The third main line diesel locomotive to be built at Crewe Works has now been in private ownership for 30 years. D5032 arrives at Pickering on the North Yorkshire Moors Railway. Brian Sharpe

D100 *Sherwood Forester* heads north from Bewdley on the Severn Valley Railway.
Brian Sharpe

Big *diesels*

It was not until 1962 that Crewe finally commenced production of diesels which, in theory at least, were in the same league as its famous Pacifics. The first 'big' diesels to be produced in quantity for BR main lines were the English-Electric Type 4 1Co-Co1s from 1958, but EE/Vulcan Foundry built these themselves.

A similar but more powerful design was the BR/Sulzer Type 4 1Co-Co1, the first 10 of which,

D1-D10, emerged from Derby in 1959 carrying British mountain names, and becoming known as the Peak class. A further development of this design, numbered from D11, commenced production at Derby but were mostly unnamed. In May 1962 though, D50 emerged from Crewe Works, the first of 88 to be built there. They were nearly all put to work on Midland Main Line services out of St Pancras, D50 later being named *The King's*

No 45055 (D84) *Royal Corps of Transport*, which is pictured on limestone hoppers at Marple in September 1984, was scrapped in 1987.
Mike Stokes Archive

Made in Crewe

No 45143 *The Royal Inniskilling Dragoon Guards*, built at Crewe as D62, passes Langstone Rock, Devon, in 1985.
The north-east-to-south-west route was a line dominated by the Class 45s and 46s in the 1970s and 1980s.
Brian Sharpe

Shropshire Light Infantry, and Crewe's last-built example, D137, acquiring the name *The Cheshire Regiment*.

It was a successful, if rather heavyweight design with a Sulzer 12-cylinder 2500hp engine and six Crompton-Parkinson nose-suspended axle-hung traction motors. Weighing in at 138tons 2cwt, the engines, which later became Class 45, produced a tractive effort of 70,000lb, considerably more than any Crewe-built steam engine.

The class was phased out of BR service in the 1980s, with the last ones being withdrawn in 1988. They have been surprisingly popular with preservationists and no less than nine of the Crewe-built engines still exist, six in regular use on heritage lines and one, No 45112 (D61) *Royal Army Ordnance Corps,* registered for main line use, based at Derby.

The Class 45s were very much a 'first-generation' design of BR diesel, and Crewe Works' next batch of diesel production was something a little more modern and glamorous, if perhaps unexpected. Just two months after D50 rolled out of the works, D1035 became the first diesel-hydraulic locomotive to be completed at Crewe.

The class 45s were always associated with the Midland Main Line.
No 45112 *The Royal Army Ordnance Corps* stands at the buffer stops at St Pancras for the very last time with a special from Derby.
Brian Sharpe

Western Class diesel at Shrewsbury in 1965. Author

Diesel–electric *v* Diesel–hydraulic
The Westerns

BR's modernisation programme was a little hasty and not all the diesel classes rushed into service were a great success. With hindsight it can be seen that one major mistake was to allow the regions to go their own way, and the Western Region which, it is said, still considered itself to be the Great Western Railway, chose hydraulic instead of electric transmission for its fleet of new diesels.

Hydraulic transmission had been standard in Germany and there was nothing wrong with the WR's choice, except that it meant that its fleet of diesels

was simply not compatible with the engines on the rest of BR. The advantage of hydraulic transmission was that a high-speed diesel engine could be used, and these are much lighter than the medium-speed engines used in the diesel-electric type 4s up to that time, which had needed two eight-wheel bogies to spread the weight. The first diesel-hydraulics were Type 4 B-Bs, with two four-wheel bogies.

However, after reasonable results from the later class of Warship diesel introduced in 1958, the WR ordered 74 bigger, better and very distinctive and stylish 2700hp C-C machines, to be known as the

Green-liveried Crewe-built Class 52 D1048 *Western Lady* departs from Goathland on the North Yorkshire Moors Railway. Brian Sharpe

Westerns. Surprisingly, although production started at
Swindon with D1000 *Western Enterprise* in 1961, it
continued simultaneously at Swindon and Crewe, with
the ex-GWR works eventually producing only 30 as
against the rival ex-LMS works at Crewe's total of 44.

They had two Maybach 1440hp diesel engines,
Voith hydraulic transmission, weighed 108 tons and
produced a tractive effort of 72,600lb. Swindon
experimented a bit with liveries, with D1000
emerging in desert sand and D1015 in golden ochre
but, although some eventually were outshopped in
standard BR Brunswick green — the GWR colour
adopted by BR for all express engines from 1951 —
most were turned out by both Crewe and Swindon in
the full glory of LMS crimson lake, by now known by
BR as maroon.

In many ways the 44 Westerns were the high point
of diesel production at Crewe Works. It was one of the
few diesel classes to have something of the style of
the express steam engines it replaced. It is perhaps
sad that the Westerns were rarely seen at Crewe in
regular service, as a diesel-hydraulic became
something of a liability once outside its normal
sphere of operation and maintenance.

The increasing unreliability of the WR
diesel-hydraulics led to their withdrawal at a
relatively early stage before they were life-expired.
While Germany's experience was good, their engines
tended to run flat-out for long periods, while the BR
ones were often just idling or ticking over and the
hydraulic transmissions did not take kindly to this
type of use. The Western hydraulics, though, certainly
had an illustrious if brief career on the WR expresses
and proved to be worthy successors to the Kings and
Castles although, by the time the last two hauled
their final train for BR in February 1977, the survivors
had been reduced to little more than pottering
around Cornwall on china clay trains.

They had one of the most fanatical enthusiasts'
followings of any BR diesel class and not only went
out with a flourish but many were saved by
preservationists. Crewe-built D1062 *Western Courier*
was the first to be preserved, and is now based on
the Severn Valley Railway. D1041 *Western Prince*
works on the East Lancashire Railway and D1048
Western Lady has seen service on the North Yorkshire
Moors Railway, but is currently under heavy overhaul
at the Midland Railway — Butterley.

Diesel workhorse – *the Class 47*

The real workhorse diesel of the 1960s was the Brush/Sulzer Type 4 Co-Co that later became universally known as the Class 47. The Brush works at Loughborough commenced production with D1500 in 1962 and built the lion's share of the 512-strong class but, once Crewe had finished its Westerns, it shared production with Brush and eventually built no less than 202 Class 47s, the last being D1111 in February 1967, coincidentally just as the works outshopped the last BR steam engine to be overhauled, Britannia Pacific No 70013 *Oliver Cromwell*.

Diesel locomotive development had now reached a stage where a medium-speed engine had been reduced in weight considerably and the civil engineer had relaxed certain restrictions on the size of wheel diameters.

The result was a refined version of the Class 45, the 12-cylinder Sulzer engine developing 2750hp and using six Brush traction motors. Weight was reduced

The Royal Train passes Winsford travelling south on the WCML on 23 May 1996 with the Class 47 locos *Prince Harry* and *Prince William* top-and-tailing. Author

No 47787 *Windsor Castle* (built at Crewe) in EWS livery brings up the rear of the Royal Train as it leaves Holyhead hauled by an older product of Crewe, No 6233 *Duchess of Sutherland.* Brian Sharpe

to 114 tons and consequently needed only six-wheel as opposed to eight-wheel bogies. They were designed to go almost anywhere and they did, eventually being seen in all corners of Britain, except the most lightly-laid or sharply-curving branch lines.

The class effectively took over all the top-link express duties on the West Coast Main Line north of Crewe and brought about the withdrawal of the Crewe-built LMS Pacifics. On paper, a Duchess could exceed the power output of a Brush Type 4 diesel, but its ability to sustain the power output was limited by the quality of the coal and the ability of the fireman. The diesel has no such limitations; it does exactly what it says on the box.

It had taken many years of diesel locomotive design and development before a class had been produced reliably and consistently to compete with British steam power at its best but, although initially slow to embrace the new technology and never at the forefront of design, Crewe Works made an important contribution to BR's modernisation.

Classified Class 47 under the TOPS renumbering system, these Type 4s have seen successive rebuildings, renumberings and new engines, and some remain in front-line service today. Both Freightliner and Virgin Trains operate the latest rebuilt reincarnations, the Class 57s, through Crewe, and many have passed to the new generation of Train Operating Companies, which use them on excursion trains in all parts of the country. They were never stylish or glamorous engines, but have been one of BR's longest-serving and most successful diesel designs.

The first Class 47 to enter preservation was No 47192, a Crewe-built example restored to original two-tone green livery as D1842. The engine is now based nearby, at the Churnet Valley Railway. Brian Sharpe

In pale blue undercoat, two Class 47s stand outside the erecting shop after overhaul. Brian Sharpe

The *works* starts to *shrink*

Class 40 No 40010 still carrying BR green livery has just entered the works for stripping in 1975. Brian Sharpe

Crewe works was rationalised and re-equipped in 1964 as steam work drew to a close. The old works and deviation area were abandoned and activity was concentrated in the steelworks area. The overall area of the works was reduced from 137 acres to 89, but it still remained the most important workshops on British Railways.

British steam railway engineering changed the face of the globe, opening it up to trade and settlement, ushering in the modern world.

For many, the beating heart of the British network was Crewe, not only a major railway junction in its own right, where four routes joined what was to become the West Coast Main Line, but its locomotive workshops were to become the biggest wholly owned by an operating company.

A Class 40 newly repainted into BR blue and a Class 47 in light blue undercoat waiting to enter the paintshop for the top coat to be applied. Brian Sharpe

A Manchester-Sheffield Woodhead route 1500v DC Bo-Bo Class 76 electric No 76034 under overhaul at Crewe in 1975. Brian Sharpe

West Coast *electrification*

Of course, the immediate effect of BR's 1955 modernisation plan was the rapid introduction of diesel locomotives, but this was always seen as merely a step towards electrification. Other countries made the transition straight from steam to electric but Britain, being a bit behind, wanted to get rid of steam quicker than it could realistically electrify.

Electrification, either AC or DC, third rail or overhead supply, had been part of the British railway scene since the start of the 20th century, but applied mainly to suburban routes with multiple-unit operation. The LNER had pioneered main line electrification, first on Teesside, then across the Pennines, at 1500v DC, mainly for heavy coal traffic, but the first full-scale

Class 86 No 86261 is lifted for the benefit of visitors during a 2003 Crewe Works open day. Author

long-distance inter-city electrification programme was the West Coast Main Line, from Euston to Birmingham, Crewe, Liverpool and Manchester.

Despite Crewe being the nerve centre of this 25kv new overhead electric railway, the works had little involvement in the design or construction of any of the locomotives and stock to be used. As with the diesels, there were initially five variations on a basic Bo-Bo design, using equipment supplied by various private manufacturers. Eventually, a standard design, the Class 86, was adopted, but construction was shared between English Electric/Vulcan Foundry and BR's Doncaster Works.

Electrification first reached Crewe from Liverpool and Manchester in 1961 and spread southwards, being completed to Euston in 1966. It was certainly a great success, but it was several years before BR took the plunge and embarked on electrifying north from Crewe, to Carlisle and Edinburgh.

When the 'Electric Scots' were finally inaugurated in 1974, it was with the assistance of a new class of 25kv Bo-Bo electrics, the Class 87, built at Crewe. There was a good reason for this. As BR was being broken down into smaller units, one of which was British Rail Engineering Ltd (BREL), and with far less locomotive building repair and maintenance now needed than in the pre-Beeching steam era, BREL had downsized quite drastically. Crewe was one of very few remaining railway workshops still able to build engines, and BREL was now in direct competition with the private contractors that had played such a vital part in modernising the railway system so quickly.

Closure of so many of the traditional locomotive workshop facilities had resulted in far more major overhauls being concentrated at the surviving works such as Crewe and Doncaster. Crewe, for example, took over jobs such as overhauling the LNER-designed 1500v DC electrics from the Manchester-Sheffield Woodhead route.

Manchester-Euston services
calling at Stockport.
No 87023 *Polmadie* on
4 July 2002 and No 87015
Howard of Effingham on
13 August 2002.
Mike Stokes Archive

Class 87, 25kv Bo-Bo electrics, built at Crewe

Liveries *are us!*

In addition to UK company styles, three EWS class 90s were painted in European liveries: French, German and Belgian.
All Author

Made in Crewe

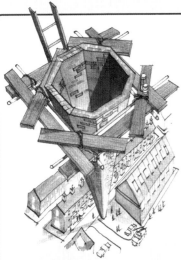

The prototype High-Speed Train with its Class 41 power cars took part in the Rail 150 celebrations at Shildon in 1975. One of the power cars is preserved in the National Railway Museum.
Brian Sharpe

Inter-City 125

Diesel locomotive construction at Crewe ceased for some years after completion of the Class 47s, but Crewe Works finally had its moment of glory in the diesel age when it built the two prototype Class 41s in 1972. These were the power cars for an entirely new concept – the High-Speed Train.

It was a simple concept. Instead of one high-powered locomotive hauling a train and running round its stock at the end of the journey, two medium-powered but fast engines were used, one at each end, controlled by one driver. The Class 41, developed at Crewe into the Class 43 HST power car,

widely introduced in 1976, was probably the most successful diesel locomotive in BR history.

The HSTs or Inter-City 125s revolutionised services on the whole of the Western Region, then the East Coast Main Line, the Midland Main Line and the cross-country routes although, like many of Crewe's products in the diesel era, they were comparatively rarely seen in the town in active service. Only now have the HSTs been partially displaced from some of these routes by electrification and new multiple-unit stock.

In the case of Virgin Trains' cross-country services, HSTs have now been replaced by Voyagers and

Crewe-built Transrail Class 56 No 56125 hurries a tank train southwards through Winsford on the WCML.
Author

Made in Crewe

Pendolinos, but HST mark two is still at very early planning stages, and Crewe's most significant contribution to the modern railway system still has many years' service ahead.

Crewe's only other diesel locomotive construction in the 1970s was when some new heavy freight diesels were ordered in 1976, although the first Class 56s were actually built in Romania. Most were built by BREL at Doncaster, but the last 20 came out of Crewe.

By 1988, the first-generation of WCML DC electrics were getting long in the tooth and a new class was introduced, again built at Crewe, the Class 90. Now the Class 81-85 and virtually all of the Class 86s, 87s and 90s have been withdrawn, although a handful of preserved examples exist.

The *High-Speed Train*

A Midland Main Line HST
passes Barrow Hill.
Brian Sharpe

The HSTs were intended to be world's fastest diesel trains and they were designed to run, if required, over 1000 miles a day. At the zenith of their career, the class accounted for approximately half the passenger miles covered by British Railways' trains. They were designed at BR Derby Works but the power cars were all manufactured at Crewe, now under British Rail Engineering Limited (BREL) between 1967 and 1982.

In total 197 power cars were built classified as Class 43. They were self-contained diesel locomotives but designed to be permanently coupled at either end of a fixed set of coaches. The first of these highly successful trains entered service in August

An Intercity-liveried HST
'flattens' the Lickey Incline.
Author

HST power car No 43167
seen receiving attention
in 'the works'.
Crewe Works Archive

1976 and, in October of that year, the Western Region of BR introduced a new high-speed timetable featuring the HSTs.

The new trains represented the first instance in a British timetable where services were timed to run at more than 100mph 'start to stop'. The trains, Paddington to Bristol and South Wales, included a leg between Swindon and Reading where they travelled at an average speed of 103.3mph. The best recorded performance of a 125 HST was in June 1973, when a train travelling between York and Northallerton achieved a speed of 143mph (232kph) and became the world's diesel traction speed record-holder.

HST sets were formed of two power cars with normally either seven or eight coaches coupled between them, and there were approximately 90 sets working regular services on the network.

39 sets	Paddington to Bristol-Cardiff-Swansea-Milford Haven-Fishguard Harbour-Cheltenham
23 sets	Aberdeen/Glasgow to Newcastle-Derby-Birmingham-Bristol-Penzance Poole to Reading-Manchester/Glasgow/Edinburgh
14 sets	St Pancras to Derby-Nottingham-Sheffield-Leeds
11 sets	King's Cross to Aberdeen-Inverness-Cleethorpes-Hull
3 sets	Euston to Holyhead

Bombardier Laira Depot at
Plymouth, where First Great
Western HST power car
No 43190 is seen being
serviced. Les Green

The HST was seen all over the network and this is No 43014 (then numbered 254025) on the Settle-Carlise route in 1978, power car No 43105 is bringing up the rear. Crewe Works Archive

The lightweight Paxman Valenta turbocharged V12 12RP200L diesel engine was chosen as the main power unit for the HSTs and that engine delivered 2250hp at 1500rpm. However, four of the class, Nos 43167, 43168, 43169 and 43170, received alternative power units in the form of Mirrlees Blackstone MB190 engines that were rated at 2400hp at 1500rpm. The fuel-carrying capacity of each unit (as built) was set at 1000 gallons and the maximum service speed allowed was 125mph (200kph). The Royal Navy uses similar Paxman Valenta engines to power both surface ships and submarines.

A feature of the HST was the absence of conventional buffers. The power cars were instead fitted with a retractable front towbar to facilitate haulage by a locomotive, and this is concealed by the stylised body shell when the unit is in normal working mode. However, some cars were fitted at a later date with a more conventional design of front buffer assembly.

Bombardier provides servicing facilities for the HSTs still running on the network, from depots at Laira, Bristol and Swansea, as well as operating works overhaul facilities for engines, cooling systems, bogie and traction motors respectively at Edinburgh, Derby and, of course, Crewe, where it all started.

Virgin-liveried HST No 43161 waits to depart Sheffield for the south in 1999. Mike Stokes Archive

Order *completed*

In 1978 the last HST vehicles to be presented to the BR board are rolled out of the Crewe erecting shops in 1978 while a section of the workforce look on.
Both Crewe Works Archive

The unique Class 89 Co-Co electric No 89001 arrives at Doncaster with a railtour from King's Cross on 4 July 1988, commemorating the 50th anniversary of *Mallard's* epic 126mph record-breaking run in 1938.
Brian Sharpe

Electric for the
East Coast

The pendulum swung the other way as, although Doncaster built many of the electric locomotives for the WCML electrification, Crewe was now in the ascendancy and built the electric locomotives for the East Coast Main Line when it was electrified.

A brave experiment was the collaboration between BREL at Crewe and Brush at Loughborough, to build a Co-Co electric suitable for heavy freight haulage over Shap and Beattock on the WCML. No 89001 never found favour, though, and was put on ECML semi-fast passenger services, for which it had not been designed. No more Class 89s were built and WCML freight is handled either by double-headed Class 86 electrics and a few more modern Class 92s, but mostly by diesels.

The ECML electric service between King's Cross, Leeds, Newcastle, Edinburgh and Glasgow has been almost exclusively in the hands of Class 91 single-ended Bo-Bos that work in push-pull mode. These state-of-the-art electric locomotives were Crewe-built in 1988-91, the last railway locomotives to be built there, and developed jointly by BREL and GEC.

Fresh out of the works, a rainy day Crewe picture of Class 91 No 91011.
Crewe Works Archive

Made in Crewe

A new Class 91 in
the test bay at Crewe.
Crewe Works Archive

Under privatisaion,
East Coat Main Line services
are operated by GNER.
A down express headed by a
Class 91 accelerates past
Werrington Junction.
Brian Sharpe

As originally built for British
Railways Inter-City, a Class
91 heads a down ECML
express up Stoke Bank at
Essendine. Brian Sharpe

Visitors to *the Works*

Over the weekend of 10-11 September 2005 the Webb Crewe Works Charity Fund staged the Great Gathering — Festival of Rail Open Weekend. Among the visiting locomotives were products of other locomotive works loaned for the occasion by the participating preserved railways.

Class 47 No 47402 Brush Traction Co-Co built in 1962 is one of 512 of this type that were originally built. Currently based at the East Lancashire Railway.

Class 45 No 45112 *The Royal Army Ordnance Corps* 1Co-Co1 built 1962 at Crewe Works, one of a total of 127 built. Operated by FM Rail Ltd. Both Author

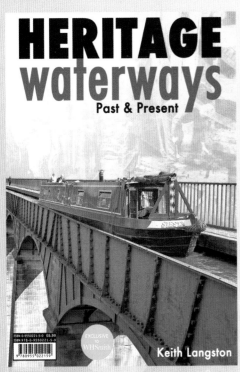
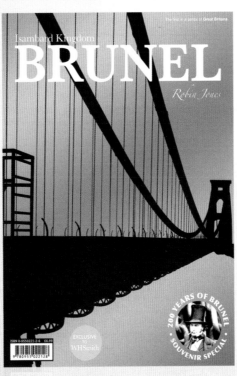

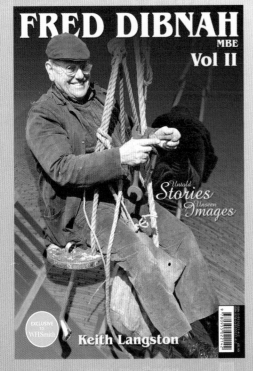

Wheel arrangements

Action shot of LMS Pacific No 6201 *Princess Elizabeth* on the 'Welsh Marches Pullman' in January 1982.
Peter J Skelton

The way that British locomotive wheel arrangements are depicted and described is taken from a system developed by the US engineer Frederic Whyte.

The Whyte System counts the wheels on both sides of an engine and shows three numbers, which are separated by dashes.

The first number gives the leading/carrying wheels, the second refers to the driving wheels and the third applies to the rear carrying wheels. The letter T after the combination denotes that it refers to a tank engine (ie a locomotive without a separate tender). The wheels on any tender attached to a locomotive form no part of the wheel arrangement notation. The two parts of an articulated locomotive are described separately and joined by a + sign.

Steam locomotives transmit all their power by way of the driving wheels, which are connected by coupling rods. The leading carrying wheels can be of a single- or double-axle arrangement and may be mounted on a bogie, a pivoted pony truck or in curved guides. The steam locomotive is by necessity a very heavy piece of machinery and, as such, it needs to be guided through curves in the track. The trailing rear carrying wheels, in addition to having a guiding function, are provided to support the weight of the firebox or, in the case of a tank engine, the coal bunker.

AS APPLIED TO STEAM LOCOMOTIVES

Several of the wheel arrangements in Frederic Whyte's notation system were also given names.

This is a selection of the common wheel arrangements used from 1923 onwards.

0-4-2	2-6-2 *Prairie*	2-8-2 *Mikado*
2-4-0	2-6-4	2-8-4 *Berkshire*
2-4-2	4-6-0 *Ten-wheeler*	4-8-0
4-4-0 *American*	4-6-2 *Pacific*	4-8-2 *Mountain*
4-4-2 *Atlantic*	4-6-4 *Hudson, Baltic*	4-8-4 *Northern*
0-6-0	0-8-0	0-10-0 *Decapod*
2-6-0 *Mogul*	2-8-0 *Consolidation*	2-10-0

Steam engines thundering through the landscape have always been a great sight to witness and experience but the industry that built, ran and maintained those leviathans did so at a large human cost.

Crewe built Stanier 8F 2-8-0 No 48305 at the
Churnet Valley Railway in 2005. David Gibson

40 years on –
the human cost

by *Les Green*

I N 2008 the rail industry will mark the 40th anniversary of the end of steam and the replacement of the last engines by the first generation of diesel and electric motive power. The last vestiges of steam will fondly be remembered by those fortunate enough to have been able to witness the last few railtours, while those dedicated to modern traction will celebrate the victory of the modernisers and the plethora of exciting new classes and engines to witness on the network.

The industry itself in 1968 could welcome substantial investment in new technologies and the brighter future that promised, and the travelling public could see an improved service, with the country at large hoping for less smog.

The 40th anniversary will no doubt attract the attention of many people in the industry, particularly in the heritage sector and the railway media but, while it will provide the opportunity to revel in nostalgia and devise events to capitalise on the potential, let us remember the human cost that these magnificent engines imposed on the working people of the industry.

Steam engines thundering through the landscape have always been a great sight to witness and experience but the industry that built, ran and maintained those leviathans did so at a large human cost.

The culture of modern industry is rightly highly attentive to all safety needs, including those of employees, but it wasn't always like that, and life in the industry that built Stanier's and Gresley's Pacifics could be hazardous and, at times, downright dangerous.

In hindsight it is easy to be critical, especially when the entire nation did not start radically to alter its ways until well into the second half of the 20th century, and the landmark Health and Safety at Work Act did not appear until the 1970s. But the attitude towards risk management and the resultant high accident rate in parts of the railway industry lagged behind other sectors of British industry.

There is some evidence of this in the privatisation of British Railways' heavy maintenance workshops as BREL in 1989, when the newly privatised company experienced considerable difficulty in finding an insurance company willing to offer employers' liability insurance, such was their record.

That particular example of poor risk management performance was subsequently tackled with vigour by successive management teams. As an example, Crewe works now has an electronic scoreboard at its main gate reminding all employees and visitors of the site's current safety record.

It is difficult to generalise but, in parts of the industry, the attitude was one of toleration of

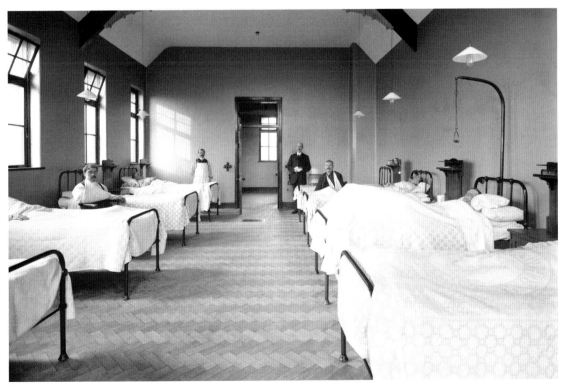

The Crewe Works hospital complete with patients, c1905.
National Railway Museum

This image from the early 1900s when viewed with modern-day safety regulations in mind just about beggars belief!
National Railway Museum

unsafe working practices, reactive rather than proactive management responses, and financial compensation as an end result of what can only be described as failure.

The railway management methods of today are a far cry from those used by the railways of earlier years. Collectively the railways are highly sensitive to the safety needs of the entire industry, including its employees; their managers are more risk-aware and therefore receptive to the advice of safety professionals. There is also a high degree of trade union involvement which includes commitment to serve on workplace committees and take part in safety inspections and audits.

The management of safety (until the last decades of the 20th century) was based on an acceptance of injuries and a reluctance to be proactive and that inevitably led to the development of a compensation culture which remained in place for many years.

Statistics produced by the post-Grouping companies demonstrated poor records although, in fairness to the railways of that time, they were part of a national culture that accepted significantly higher levels of industrial accidents and related diseases.

There may be many debates about the speed at which the industry adopted a good safety culture but the fact remains that railway engineering and the operation of trains is, of its essence, heavy mechanical and electrical engineering with incumbent risk levels that few other industries have to endure and manage.

Taking as an example the LMS (London Midland & Scottish), the biggest railway company between the

two world wars, in reported accidents for 1929 it had in 'movement accidents' 75 employees killed and 1,270 with serious injuries out of a workforce of approximately 245,000, which represented 38 per cent of the industry's total workforce. A further 21 'other' people were apparently killed. As they were not passengers or trespassers we can only assume that they were contractors' staff.

However, in the category 'non-movement' accidents for the same year, a further 20 employees were killed and 6,279 injured, while the 'other persons' category fared a little better with only four

Molten metal being poured in the Crewe Works foundry c1905; notice the absence of any protective clothing.
National Railway Museum

killed and 214 injured. The total cost in human life was 120. Incredibly, these figures do not include railway workshops or factories, so the accident rates at massive works like Derby and Crewe were ignored for reporting purposes.

Through the 1930s the figures did improve at the LMS and, by 1936, with employee numbers at 222,000, deaths had fallen to a reported 113. These figures have to be read only as a guide because, at that time, the real effects of industrial disease from materials like asbestos and oils with carcinogenic effects were then not fully understood.

In total the railway industry recorded the deaths of 3,391 employees and contractors for the five years between 1929 and 1936 (figures for 1930-31 were not reported for some reason).

There are many books on the history of railways referring to inherent risks and dubious working practices, but the first-hand experience of Charles Taylor, who served his apprenticeship in Crewe Works, are an illustration of the risks employees had to endure to put trains on the tracks.

Mr Taylor's book, *Life in a Loco Works,* is a study of his journey through the different departments of the

In this early 1900s picture of a Crewe Works machine shop locomotive axles are being worked on while the foreman, resplendent in his 'blocker' (bowler hat), looks on. National Railway Museum

works during his apprenticeship in the Second World War years. The most incredible feature is that, despite all his references to the end result of poor safety management, such as the 'compo cases' (of which you will hear more later), the extent of the workshops' safety awareness was the issue of 'a red book on safety' on his first day! You may wonder how many red books went unread!

Taylor throughout the book readily accepts the daily reality of possible serious injury and refers to many staff who had lost fingers, hands, arms, legs and, in particular, eyes, as compensation cases, whose lot in life appeared to be to undertake permanent light duties.

The definition of light duties, however, may not be in accord with our own as one poor soul who had, in Taylor's words, 'one arm and a hook', was on duties that required him to throw ash into a high-sided vehicle with a long-handled shovel!

In one department of eight workers where Taylor was employed, four were in the unfortunate position of having lost an eye. The loss of eyes did not appear to be restricted to Crewe for, in 1941, a worker in York Works was given an instruction to return to his old job as an 'angle straightener' following an accident in which he lost an eye and had later been certified fit 'to resume work in a position where the left eye will not be endangered' (*The Life and Times of York Carriage Works*). So much for eye protection!

In an age before the introduction of the National Health Service, Taylor was complimentary about the hospital treatment provided by the railway after injury or illness, with hospital funds, accident funds and five convalescent homes to look after staff, and this may well have been a significant improvement on many other industries of the day.

One aspect that figures highly in the daily thoughts of workers was the risk of having to see the works doctor, Dr Moore, who apparently had certain skills in the treatment of 'mangled fingers and blackened nails'. On Taylor's visit with a steel splinter embedded in a finger, Dr Moore was overheard to say to the nurse on duty: "Hold his finger and turn his head away." Taylor soon knew why!

Another daily hazard in the male-dominated workshop was 'boys being boys', and practical jokes resulted in some hairy moments, but Taylor was quickly brought into line with a sharp 'clip round the ear' from a one-eyed operator who, on catching his young apprentice propelling steel balls at a considerable rate of knots across the workshop by striking them with a hammer, explained that he had already lost one eye and was not about to lose another. Corporal punishment from peers and elders was normal for minor offences committed in the workplace until recent times.

The payment system, which had a strong piecework, or payment by results, element embodied in it could also add to the risks workers would take. To improve a weekly wage packet, and in the absence of a firm safety culture, shortcuts on safe working practices were tempting.

With injuries commonplace, the medical centres were well-equipped and manned, and to this day some of that equipment has been retained; a favourite trick of the medical staff at Crewe on open days is to display the site's standard amputation kit, bone saw and all, for the shock and horror of the visitors.

Made in Crewe

The potentially dangerous
working conditions are clearly
seen in this archive picture of
a Crewe Works machine
shop. There are a great many
unguarded drive belts and
work pieces on the shop floor.
National Railway Museum

A busy machine shop is seen
in this 1905 picture.
Note the clutter of work
pieces on the floor around
the machinists, something
that would never be allowed
today. National Railway Museum

Taylor refers to commonplace injuries and the role of the medical centres but then goes on to say that there was 'the occasional death on duty to cope with' and explains his personal knowledge of two incidents where death occurred.

The first case was that of a labourer who had merely been pushing a truck, which sounds innocuous enough except that the truck had on it two large castings for the repair of one of LNWR's 'Super Ds'. The castings had not been properly secured and when one fell striking a luckless worker it killed him outright.

The second death was seen by a woman in a nearby housing estate who, when watching shunting operations from a window in her house, saw a man fall to his death under a wagon. She was told later in the day that the dead man was her own husband!

More than one railway town possessed its own orphanage specifically for those created by the railway industry. Crewe had the Webb Orphanage established by a legacy in the will of the great engineer Frank Webb, and Derby had St Christopher's.

The people of Crewe had a cruel reminder of the death rate on the railway because the orphans were frequently seen around the town in their standard uniform of a brown jumper with the yellow initial WO embroidered in yellow. Designer labels railway-style!

If there was insufficient action on basic prevention methods — and in Taylor's book he says that Crewe did not even provide eye protection — then there was nothing done to prevent long-term damage to employee health caused by the processes and materials involved.

Damage to hearing was probably the most widespread effect on employees' health from the processes involved, and in this the railways were little different from many other industries with the result that claims for industrial deafness were commonplace among workers in the industry.

Today best practice prevails, audiometric testing and screening is routine and ear defenders are readily available in all shops where necessary. On privatisation in 1989, BREL offered every employee a hearing test to establish the basic level of damage done to employees in the nationalised period and, as a result, the claims for damage poured into the solicitors' offices.

Dermatitis cases caused by oils and greases have been common and, more recently, the link between these materials and testicular cancer has been a subject of staff awareness campaigns, but by far the most dangerous material to have a long-term effect on the workforces of latter years was asbestos.

Taylor uses an expression 'asbestos was king' to summarise how widespread its use was in the railway industry and how glass fibre was rejected as an insulating material by the staff in the 1930s because it irritated the skin. Little did they know how asbestos would irritate their lungs with such devastating effects?

Deaths caused by asbestos are, to this day, a commonplace occurrence in the workshop towns, and all who worked with the material or close to it know that they, too, are at risk.

The following may come as a shock to those who admire the splendid sight of a Stanier locomotive painted in crimson lake or a King in GWR green because below the boiler casing and wrapped all around the boiler was blue asbestos and the lagging on all pipes was white asbestos.

Furthermore asbestos pastes were mixed by hand; and blue and white asbestos for packing were

nixed together in a propriety brand called Bestobel. One single fibre invisible to the naked eye was sufficient after a period of some 20 years' gestation to kill after a relatively short period of time – and here is no cure.

Early classes of diesels were also heavily reliant on asbestos for insulation and even today there remains in regular use an asbestos removal facility t Crewe works. Needless to say, nothing is left to hance and the standard of exposure is nil.

Another health problem suffered by many workers in the workshops and possibly on the civil ngineering sections is that caused by the umulative effects of using percussion and vibrating ools for long periods –vibration white finger.

This is an industrial disease that affects ndividuals differently according to their individual usceptibility to the equipment used. Its symptoms ange from mere tingling in the fingers and some ain on cold mornings to potential gangrene and oss of fingers.

Erecting shop workers in particular, were prone to his industrial injury but frequently suffered in ilence as a visit to the works doctor could result in medical restriction and fear of job loss or a ransfer to component overhaul that did not match he job satisfaction of working on railway vehicles.

Railway work has had its many rewards and, while it is not the highest-paid occupation, the lose comradeship of workmates and the job atisfaction of being a part of a high-profile ndustry, combined with high level of personal esponsibility and skill, have their appeal.

But such was the cost in human life that it moved lassic Victorian writer Charles Dickens to tell an udience the remuneration of railwaymen met only the 'ordinary wants of life' in exchange for risks that cost the lives of one railway worker in every 2000. Conversely the travelling passenger was only at risk in a ratio of one in eight-million. Railways have always had a good passenger safety record.

It was no surprise, given the high level of death and injury, that some of the great names in Victorian society came together in 1858 to help launch the Railway Benevolent Institute, now the Railway Benefit Fund, to support permanently incapacitated railway servants and widows left in distress.

Charles Dickens, Joseph Locke MP, the Prince of Wales and later Queen Victoria were all to offer their support in one way or another during the 19th century, and in the 20th century the charity could list Churchill and the Queen Mother among its supporters and patrons.

Despite the demise of the railway industry, the legacy of the past is still there and the needs of incapacitated staff and widows remain basically the same as those of 148 years ago; the Railway Benevolent Fund is still there to help them.

The fund, based in Crewe, has assumed the responsibility of now-defunct charities such as the Webb Orphans' Fund and supports orphans and children of railway families suffering hardship. Despite the welfare state and a better-paid and cared-for society, there are still many retired and working railway people who, for various reasons, require financial support and, in 2005, almost £400,000 was dispersed to railway people needing help.

While so much is different from the time when Charles Dickens raised his voice in the middle of the 19th century, in another sense nothing has changed.

Early classes of diesels were also heavily reliant on asbestos for insulation and even today there remains in regular use an asbestos removal facility at Crewe works. In this line up of diesel power at the 'works' is class 47 locomotive belonging to FM Rail. No 47832 was named *Driver Tom Clark O.B.E.*, at the Great Gathering in September 2005 in honour of the legendary Crewe footplateman.

Note. *Les Green retired from his position as Human Resources Director at Bombardier's Crewe site in 2005 after serving at the 'works' for just over 16 years. Les is currently the chairman of the Webb Crewe Works Charity Fund committee.*

REGISTERED CHARITY No 206312 - THE RAILWAY BENEVOLENT INSTITUTION
For more information contact www.railwaybenefitfund.org.uk or phone 01270 251316

the RAILWAY BENEFIT FUND

The Railway Benevolent Institution (RBI) came into existence in 1858 following proposals 'to provide some form of care and financial aid to needy railway personnel' and 'to establish an institution for necessitous railway children'. Railway employment was very dangerous at that time and there was virtually no social provision as we know it now.

Initially, pressure came from clerks and junior officers but, at the first general meeting on 8 May 1858, they willingly gave way to a managing committee consisting of top railway company chairmen and managers. At an early meeting on 16 March 1859, the chairman, Joseph Locke MP, said he hoped the railways would combine to support 'this most excellent and valuable institution'.

Progress was slow, especially in terms of financial support from within the railway because junior staff could not afford to subscribe even a guinea a year from wages, which were not fashioned to provide help for others in time of need. Some income was obtained through annual dinners. The Marquess of Lansdowne, William Cubitt, the Duke of Devonshire and the Prince of Wales, as presidents of the institution, chaired these occasions, as did Charles Dickens in 1867. He drew particular attention to the debt owed by the industry and travellers to railway staff in their hazardous and dangerous employment and he sought support for their welfare.

In succeeding years the RBI has pursued the same aims and has enjoyed support from the public, all grades of staff by voluntary paybill deduction, the trade unions and management. Great help has been given to its beneficiaries in the form of annuities for retired staff and widows in financial need. These include special grants to railway people in immediate distress or in need of equipment to overcome various forms of disability, help to railway families, assistance to staff currently employed who are injured while at work or who fall ill, payments to elderly people to enable them to continue to live in their own homes and educational training, and everyday living grants to needy railway children.

Large numbers are helped each year at substantial expenditure. For example, during 2000 just under 2000 people received over £1-million. The fall in the markets following 9/11 greatly reduced the income of the RBI and, during 2005, it was able to help only 850 people with grants totalling almost £440,000.

All the recent chairmen of the former British Railways Board have been presidents of the institution. The current president is Sir William McAlpine.

Today the RBI is managed by a board of active and retired senior railway managers, including a number from the new train operating companies and Network Rail. Thus its traditions have continued from its inception and its benefits are still available to railway staff, their families and dependants, whether they are active or retired.

Her Late Majesty, Queen Elizabeth the Queen Mother, was patron of the RBI for 63 years and always took a great deal of interest in the affairs of the institution.

The RBI was relaunched on the 28 February 2006 under the name of Railway Benefit Fund, a name more in keeping with the 21st century.